First World War
and Army of Occupation
War Diary
France, Belgium and Germany

36 DIVISION
Divisional Troops
173 Brigade Royal Field Artillery.
27 November 1915 - 20 February 1919

WO95/2496/6

The Naval & Military Press Ltd
www.nmarchive.com
Published in association with The National Archives

Published by

The Naval & Military Press Ltd

Unit 10 Ridgewood Industrial Park,

Uckfield, East Sussex,

TN22 5QE England

Tel: +44 (0) 1825 749494

www.naval-military-press.com

www.nmarchive.com

This diary has been reprinted in facsimile from the original. Any imperfections are inevitably reproduced and the quality may fall short of modern type and cartographic standards.

© **Crown Copyright**
Images reproduced by permission of The National Archives, London, England, 2015.

Contents

Document type	Place/Title	Date From	Date To
Heading	WO95/2496/6		
Heading	36th Division 173rd Brigade R.F.A. Nov 1915-Feb 1919 (Jly-Sep 1917 Diaries Are Missing)		
Heading	36 Div 173rd Bde: R.F.A. Vol I		
War Diary	Bordon	27/11/1915	27/11/1915
War Diary	Havre	28/11/1915	28/11/1915
War Diary	Vauchelles Les-Domart	29/11/1915	31/12/1915
Heading	36th Div. 173rd Bde: R.F.A. Vol ; 2		
War Diary	Norbecourt	01/12/1915	31/12/1915
Heading	173rd Bde: R.F.A. Vol : 3		
War Diary	Vauchelle-Les-Domart	01/01/1916	23/01/1916
War Diary	Boismont	24/01/1916	24/01/1916
War Diary	Nouveau-Brighton	25/01/1916	22/02/1916
War Diary	On The March	24/02/1916	28/02/1916
War Diary	Engelbelmer	29/02/1916	29/02/1916
Heading	173 R F A Vol 5		
Heading	29 17 Bde R F A Vol		
War Diary	Englebelmer	01/03/1916	26/04/1916
War Diary	Martinsart	29/04/1916	30/04/1916
Miscellaneous	Off F.A. G.S Office The Base	02/06/1916	02/06/1916
War Diary	Martinsart	01/06/1916	16/06/1916
War Diary	Martin	16/05/1916	23/05/1916
War Diary	Martinsart and Mesnil	24/05/1916	31/05/1916
Heading	36th Divisional Artillery. 173rd Brigade Royal Field Artillery June 1916		
Miscellaneous	Officer O/C D.A.G.S. Office The Base.	14/08/1916	14/08/1916
War Diary	Martinsart	01/06/1916	20/06/1916
War Diary	Mesnil Martinsart	20/06/1916	24/06/1916
War Diary	Mesnil	25/06/1916	30/06/1916
Heading	36th Divisional Artillery. 173rd Brigade Royal Field Artillery July 1916		
War Diary	Mesnil Valley	01/07/1916	05/07/1916
War Diary	Mesnil	02/07/1916	05/07/1916
War Diary	Aveluy	06/07/1916	31/07/1916
War Diary	Neuve Eglise Hill 63	01/08/1916	31/08/1916
Miscellaneous	Appendix "A"		
Miscellaneous	Appendix A		
Heading	War Diary of 173rd Bde R.F.A. Period 1st To 30th September 1916 Vol. I		
War Diary	Neuve Eglise And Hill 63	01/09/1916	09/09/1916
War Diary	Neuve Eglise	09/09/1916	11/09/1916
War Diary	Dranoutre	11/09/1916	30/09/1916
Operation(al) Order(s)	36th Divisional Artillery Order No. 12 Appendix "A"	04/09/1916	04/09/1916
Operation(al) Order(s)	Reference Map 28 5 W 1 1/10000. Left Group Order No. 2 Appendix "E"	27/09/1916	27/09/1916
Miscellaneous	Appendix B	17/09/1916	17/09/1916
Miscellaneous	Left Group 36th Divisional Artillery Appendix B	17/09/1916	17/09/1916
Operation(al) Order(s)	Left Group Operation Order No. 1 Appendix "D"	20/09/1916	20/09/1916
Miscellaneous	Bombardment Of Front Line, N.36.D 7005-N36.D. 5740 On 6th September, 1916	06/09/1916	06/09/1916

Miscellaneous	Appendix B	15/09/1916	15/09/1916
Miscellaneous	Appendix B		
Operation(al) Order(s)	Left Group Order No. 3 Appendix "F"	29/09/1916	29/09/1916
Heading	War Diary of 173 Brigade R.F.A. 36 Division For October 1916 Vol 12		
War Diary	Dranoutre	01/10/1916	31/10/1916
Operation(al) Order(s)	Amendment To Left Group Operation Order No. 6 Appx B	08/10/1916	08/10/1916
Operation(al) Order(s)	Left Group Supplementary Order to Operation Order No. 6 Appendix "B"	08/10/1916	08/10/1916
Operation(al) Order(s)	Left Group Order No. 6 Appendix B	05/10/1916	05/10/1916
Operation(al) Order(s)	Left Group 2/5th Div Arty Operation Order No. 9 Appendix C		
Operation(al) Order(s)	Left Group Order Appendix "D"		
Operation(al) Order(s)	Left Group Order No. 12 Appendix "E"	28/10/1916	28/10/1916
Operation(al) Order(s)	Left Group Order No. 11 Appendix "F"	28/10/1916	28/10/1916
Operation(al) Order(s)	Left Group Order No. 5 Appendix "A"	11/10/1916	11/10/1916
Heading	War Diary For 173rd Brigade, R.F.A. Month Ending Nov. 30. 1916 Vol. 13		
War Diary	Dranoutre	01/11/1916	30/11/1916
Operation(al) Order(s)	Left Group Order No. Appendix "A"		
Operation(al) Order(s)	Left Group Order No. 15 Appendix B	14/11/1916	14/11/1916
Operation(al) Order(s)	Left Group Order No. 14 Appendix "C"	10/11/1916	10/11/1916
Operation(al) Order(s)	Ammendment No. 1 To Left Group Order No. 16 Appendix "D"	22/11/1916	22/11/1916
Operation(al) Order(s)	Left Group Order No. 16	21/11/1916	21/11/1916
Heading	War Diary 173rd Brigade. R.F.A. 36th Division December 1st. 1916 To 31st 1916 Vol 14		
War Diary	Dranoutre	01/12/1916	29/12/1916
War Diary	March To Calais Area	30/12/1916	31/12/1916
Operation(al) Order(s)	Spanbroek Group Order No. 2 Appendix A	25/12/1916	25/12/1916
Heading	War Diary 173rd Brigade, R.F.A. 36th Division Vol 15		
War Diary		01/01/1917	15/01/1917
War Diary	Neuve Eglise	16/01/1917	27/01/1917
War Diary	English Farm	27/01/1917	31/01/1917
Operation(al) Order(s)	36th Divisional Artillery Order No. 48	11/01/1917	11/01/1917
Miscellaneous	Programme Of Bombardment		
Operation(al) Order(s)	Right Group Order No. 1	17/01/1917	17/01/1917
Heading	War Diary 173rd Bde. R.F.A. 36th Division. Vol 16		
War Diary	English Farm	01/02/1917	17/03/1917
War Diary	Little Kemmel	17/03/1917	31/03/1917
War Diary		01/04/1917	11/04/1917
War Diary	Little Kemmel	12/04/1917	27/05/1917
War Diary	N 25 G 81	27/05/1917	28/05/1917
War Diary	N 26 D 07	29/05/1917	31/05/1917
War Diary	N 26 C 9.6	01/06/1917	06/06/1917
War Diary	Regent St Dugouts	07/06/1917	20/06/1917
War Diary	St Jans Cappel	21/06/1917	26/06/1917
War Diary	Regent St Dugouts	27/06/1917	30/06/1917
Heading	Jly-Sep 1917 Missing		
War Diary	P 4 O 85 80	10/10/1917	25/10/1917
War Diary	P 4 A 8.8	01/11/1917	02/11/1917
War Diary	Bertincourt	03/11/1917	19/11/1917
War Diary	K 25 A 3.0	20/11/1917	20/11/1917
War Diary	Demicourt	26/11/1917	30/11/1917
War Diary	R 25 A 3.0	20/11/1917	20/11/1917

Type	Description	Start	End
War Diary	Demicourt	21/11/1917	03/12/1917
War Diary	Beaumetz	04/12/1917	05/12/1917
War Diary	I 12 b	06/12/1917	12/12/1917
War Diary	Havrincourt Wood	12/12/1917	13/12/1917
War Diary	Beaucamp	14/12/1917	25/12/1917
War Diary	Beaulencourt	26/12/1917	31/12/1917
War Diary	Buire	01/01/1918	01/01/1918
War Diary	Hamel	02/01/1918	07/01/1918
War Diary	Lequesnel	07/01/1918	11/01/1918
War Diary	Roisglise	11/01/1918	13/01/1918
War Diary	Happencourt	13/01/1918	31/01/1918
War Diary	A 30 G 08	01/02/1918	13/02/1918
War Diary	Grand Seraucourt	14/02/1918	16/02/1918
War Diary	G 14 G. 8	21/02/1918	28/02/1918
Heading	36th Divisional Artillery. 173rd Brigade R.F.A. March 1918 Appendices Attached :) Account Of Operations 21st-31st Barrage Tables Artillery Instructions Targets.		
War Diary	G.14.G. 2.8	01/03/1918	19/03/1918
War Diary	G. 8 A. 1.2	20/03/1918	21/03/1918
Miscellaneous	O.C. A, B, C, And D/, 175 A/153 App I	02/03/1918	02/03/1918
Miscellaneous	O.C. A/173. B/173. C/173. D/173. App II	02/03/1918	02/03/1918
Miscellaneous	O.C. A/173 B/173 C/173 D/173 App III	04/03/1918	04/03/1918
Miscellaneous	Target App V		
Miscellaneous	O.C. A/173 B/173 C/173 D/173	08/03/1918	08/03/1918
Miscellaneous	O.C. A/173 B/173 C/173 D/173 App VI	11/03/1918	11/03/1918
Miscellaneous	Barrage to Coverline of Resistance		
Miscellaneous	O.C. /173 173rd Brigade No. D 116/25 App VII	11/03/1918	11/03/1918
Miscellaneous	O.C. A, B, C, And D/173 O.C. 383, 463, 463, And 461 Batteries 2/Lieut Fagan R.H App VIII	12/03/1918	12/03/1918
Miscellaneous	O.C. A/173 B/173 C/173 D/173 App. IX	13/03/1918	13/03/1918
Miscellaneous	O.C. A/173. B/173. C/173. D/173. App IV	07/03/1918	07/03/1918
Miscellaneous	Right Group		
Miscellaneous	O.C. A/173 B/173 C/173 D/173 App. X	13/03/1918	13/03/1918
Miscellaneous	Inter-Group Reinforcing Barrages. In Case Of Attack On Front Held By 107th Inf. Brigade.		
Miscellaneous	Inter-Group Reinforcing Barrages In Case Of Attack On Front Held BY 108th Inf. Brigade.		
Miscellaneous	Right Group Mutual Support.		
Miscellaneous	O.C. C/173 D/173. 173rd Brigade R.F.A. No. M 78/13 App. XI	17/03/1918	17/03/1918
Miscellaneous	O.C. A/173 B/173 C/173 C/173 Forward Position App XII	19/03/1918	19/03/1918
Miscellaneous	Barrage Table		
Miscellaneous	Right Group 36th Divisional Artillery App XIII		
Miscellaneous	Appendix 13 Immediately Follows War Diary.		
Heading	36th Divisional Artillery. 173rd Brigade R.F.A. April 1918		
War Diary		01/04/1918	30/04/1918
War Diary	173rd Brigade R.F.A. 36th Division		
War Diary		01/05/1918	31/05/1918
War Diary	173rd Brigade R F.A 36th Division II Corps II Army.		
War Diary		01/06/1918	30/06/1918
War Diary	173rd Brigade R.F.A. 36th Division Xth Corps II Army.		
War Diary		01/07/1918	30/07/1918

Miscellaneous	173rd Brigade R.F.A. 36th Division Xth Corps Second Army.		
War Diary		01/08/1918	31/08/1918
Miscellaneous	173 Bde R.F.A. 36.Division X Corps		
War Diary		01/09/1918	30/09/1918
Miscellaneous	173rd Brigade R.F.A. X Corps 36 Division.		
War Diary		01/10/1918	20/02/1919

WO95/24996

36TH DIVISION

173RD BRIGADE R.F.A.

NOV 1915-FEB 1919

(JLY - SEP 1917 DIARIES ARE MISSING)

1/3rd Bde: R.F.A.
Vol: I

Nov 17-30
Dec

Nov. 15
to
Feb. 19
(Feb - Sep 1917 Missing)

36th Dn

Army Form C. 2118.

173rd Bde R.F.A.

WAR DIARY
INTELLIGENCE SUMMARY.
(Erase heading not required.)

Instructions regarding War Diaries and Intelligence Summaries are contained in F.S. Regs., Part II and the Staff Manual respectively. Title pages will be prepared in manuscript.

Place	Date	Hour	Summary of Events and Information	Remarks and references to Appendices
Bordon	27.11.15		The Brigade began to entrain at various hours at BORDON and LIPHOOK. Rules to SOUTHAMPTON. Embarked on S.S. SOUTH-WEST MILLER and ARCHIMEDES.	
Havre	28.11.15		Crossed the CHANNEL and disembarked at HAVRE in the morning. Entrained at various hours.	
Vauchelles les-Domart	29.11.15		Detrained at PONT REMY in the morning and proceeded by route march to VAUCHELLES-les-DOMART where the men were close billeted and horses and guns put out in the open. Halted.	
Do	30.11.15		No occurrences calling for any special remark took place during the movie, or subsequently.	

R.H. ...thy.
Lt. Col.
Comdg 173rd Bde R.F.A.

2353 Wt. W2544/1454 700,000 5/15 D.D.&L. A.D.S.S./Forms/C. 2118.

Army Form C. 2118.

173 Bde. R.F.A.

WAR DIARY
INTELLIGENCE SUMMARY.
(Erase heading not required.)

Instructions regarding War Diaries and Intelligence Summaries are contained in F. S. Regs., Part II. and the Staff Manual respectively. Title pages will be prepared in manuscript.

Place	Date	Hour	Summary of Events and Information	Remarks and references to Appendices
VAUCHELLE-ls-DOMART	1.12.15.		Brigade halted. "D" Battery moved to and billetted in the village of MOUFLERS.	
Do	2.12.15 to 8.12.15		Brigade halted. Continued training and began to build winter horse lines and improve the condition of the billets in the village. Very little training done.	
Do	9.12.15		Ammunition Column moved to VILLERS-SOUS-AILLY	
Do	10.12.15		"A" Battery moved to MOUFLERS.	
Do	14.12.15		All training suspended and all hands put to building winter horse standings.	26
Do.	15.12.15 to 31.12.15		This work has continued. No occurrences calling for any special remarks took place during the month.	

P. Wheatley
Lt. Col.
Commdg 173 Bde R.F.A.

173 w Bde: R Pa.
vol: 2

WAR DIARY
or
INTELLIGENCE SUMMARY.
(Erase heading not required.)

Army Form C. 2118.

Place	Date	Hour	Summary of Events and Information	Remarks and references to Appendices
MORBECOURT	Dec. 1st.		Routine. It should have been stated earlier that the 20th and 44th Trench Mortar Batteries which were transferred to the 24th Divisional Artillery on the 24th October are now a regular portion of the Artillery. Each battery has half its personnel and all its guns in the trenches, while half the personnel are in rest billets. The personnel in the trenches draw supplies from the Infantry. The personnel in rest billets are attached: 20th T.M.Battery to 106th B.A.C. 44th T.M.Battery to 107th B.A.C.	
	2nd.		Lieut.Farming (Bedford Regt.) joined as O.C.T.M.Batteries. Billeting parties sent to OLERQUES,AUDREHEM,JOURNY and ALQUINES.	
	3rd.		108th.F.A.Bde moved to ALQUINES. and JOURNY.	
	4th.		109th.F.A.Bde (less C/109.)moved to CLERQUES. 194th Co.A.S.C. placed under C.R.A.for administration and discipline. Routine. ON formation of 131st Howitzer Bde C/109th + 1 Sub.109th B.A.C.,13 O.R.and 3 full teams of D.A.C.were transferred to 2nd Canadian Division.	
	5th.		C/109th + Sub B.A.C.marched via CASSELL to BERTHEN,halting at BROXEELE.	

Instructions regarding War Diaries and Intelligence Summaries are contained in F. S. Regs., Part II. and the Staff Manual respectively. Title pages will be prepared in manuscript.

Army Form C. 2

WAR DIARY
or
INTELLIGENCE SUMMARY.
(Erase heading not required.)

Instructions regarding War Diaries and Intelligence Summaries are contained in F. S. Regs., Part II. and the Staff Manual respectively. Title pages will be prepared in manuscript.

Place	Date	Hour	Summary of Events and Information	Remarks and references to Appendices
NORT BECOURT	Dec 5th		for the night. 5th 1st D.A.C. Staff marched to CAMPAGNE near St. OMER.	
	6th		Routine.	
			Report on billeting reconnaissance sent in to Fd Gr. Inlays. TOURNEHEM, ZOUAFQUES	
	7th		BONNINGUES. Found each available for an artillery Bde, and SUSMY for a battery.	
	8th		Routine. Capt V.A.H. TAYLOR cmd from 1st Div and takes command of B/107.	
	9th		Routine.	
	10th		Routine.	
			Following Officers attached 2 Lt J.T Mito to 104th Bde	
			H. Thomas - 103 -	
			J.L. Miller - 107 -	
			S.J. King - 108 -	
			MSH Smith - 108 -	
			J. Howatta - 109 -	
			K.S. WR - 109 -	
	11th		Routine. Motor car Bde down sent to WATTEN for repair. C.R.A. inspected 107 Bde R.F.A	
	12th		Routine.	
	13th		C.R.A. w/106 & 104th Bde R.H.A.	
	14th		C.R.A. inspected 108th Bde R.F.A.	
	15th		Routine.	
	16		Capt B A Gilpin R.FA comdg 21st Div A.C. has been posted to command 108 B.A.C.	

2353 Wt. W 5144/1454 700,000 5/15 D. D. & L. A.D.S.S./Forms/C. 2118.

Army Form C. 2118

WAR DIARY
or
INTELLIGENCE SUMMARY.

(Erase heading not required.)

Instructions regarding War Diaries and Intelligence Summaries are contained in F. S. Regs., Part II. and the Staff Manual respectively. Title pages will be prepared in manuscript.

Place	Date	Hour	Summary of Events and Information	Remarks and references to Appendices
NORTBECOURT	Aug 17		Major General So Kavak Plumer issued 2nd Army orders No 27 Dec AS	
	Aug 18		Routine	
	19		Routine	
	20		Routine. B.S.M.E met 103rd Bde R.F.A. appointed 2nd Lieutenant, promoted to Capt.	
	21		Two officers sent to survey school at BERGUES	
	22		Routine	
	23		Routine	
	24		Routine	
	25		Routine. Roll "A" now few men.	
	26		Routine. Roll "A" now few men.	
	27		Move cancelled	
	28		Routine	
	29		Routine. Capt V.A.H. Taylor 107th Brigade R.F.A. evacuated. Personnel 63 Bty h.Q. Staff move to HONDSPETHE 107 Brigade march to HONDSPETHE	
	30		Office moved to STEENVOORDE. 107 Brigade moved into TEENVOORDE	
	31		One of Gun officers 107 Bde move to suspension of Brigade to Ducauwalen	
			Commands D.Group 107 Bde move to 25 Bde again arrangements made	
			10 Bde 107 Brigade are now in STEENVOORDE area	
			Staff 106 Bde officers 106 Bde move to 19 Bde & agreement	
			107 Bde now to 63 R.F.A. Bde Margot town	

173d Mdc. R.P.a.
Vol: 3

36.

Army Form C. 2118.

173 Bde. R.F.A.

WAR DIARY
INTELLIGENCE SUMMARY.
(Erase heading not required.)

Place	Date	Hour	Summary of Events and Information	Remarks and references to Appendices
VAUCHELLE les-Domart	1.1.16 to 9.1.16		Brigade halted and not continued or units horse-standings	
Do	10.1.16 to 23.1.16		Standings being practically completed Brigade resumed its training	
BOISMONT	24.1.16		Brigade marched and billeted for the night at the villages of BOISMONT and MONS	
NOUVEAU-BRIGHTON	25.1.16		Brigade marched in 2 its new training ground by the Sea & billeted at the villages of NOUVEAU-BRIGHTON and MOLLIERE.	
Do	26.1.16 to 31.1.16		Continued training.	
			No occurrence calling for any special remark took place during the month.	

P. Wheatley. Lt. Col.
Comdg. 173 Bde. R.F.A.

Army Form C. 2118.

173 Bde R.F.A.

WAR DIARY
INTELLIGENCE SUMMARY.
(Erase heading not required.)

Places	Date	Hour	Summary of Events and Information	Remarks and references to Appendices
NOUVEAU BRIGHTON	1.2.16 to 22.2.16		Brigade continued training. Some practice carried out near CAYEUX beginning on 14.2.16 and each battery fired some 100 rounds.	
On the March	24.2.16 to 29.2.16		Brigade marched up to line to take over gun position held by II 32nd Brigade R.F.A. of 4th Divisional Artillery (attached to 36th Division)	
ENGELBELMER	29.2.16		Brigade began to take over gun positions etc. "A" and "C" Batts about 1000 x from Engelbelmer. "B" in Engelbelmer. "D" not yet arrived being marched up in Company with 153 Bde R.F.A. Bde. H.Q. at ACHEUX.	

R. Shuttleworth Lt. Col.
Comdg 173 Bde R.F.A.

173 RFA
Vol 5

29

17 Bde - R 7a
———————
Vol

WAR DIARY
INTELLIGENCE SUMMARY

173 Bde. R.F.A. Army Form C. 2118.

Place	Date	Hour	Summary of Events and Information	Remarks and references to Appendices
ENGELBELMER	1.3.16 to		Headquarters of Brigade established at ENGELBELMER. Batteries continued taking up positions at sector at a time. "B" Battery arrived on 3.3.16 and took up gun position (in section only) at AUCHONVILLERS.	

WAR DIARY

INTELLIGENCE SUMMARY.

(Erase heading not required.)

173 Bde R.F.A. Army Form C. 2118.

Place	Date	Hour	Summary of Events and Information	Remarks and references to Appendices
ENGLEBELMER	1.3.16		Headquarters of Brigade established at ENGLEBELMER. Batteries continued taking up positions, a section at a time. "B" Battery arrived on 3.3.16 and took over gun position (one section only) at AUCHONVILLERS.	
	5.3.16		Taking over complete at 9 am and 4 Divisional Artillery moved out.	
	6.3.16 to 31.3.16		During remainder of the month there was no military trench warfare. Neither British nor German attempted any special offensive. There was occasional burst bombardment and retaliation. Each battery fired 100 – 150 rounds perfecting wire cutting, registration, making practice shells etc. etc. Guns calibrated, enemy's new batteries were checked. Total no. of rounds fired during the month was Shrapnel 2143 H.E. 859. There were no casualties during the month. P.B. Wadley Major. Comdg. 173 Bde R.F.A.	

WAR DIARY

173 Bde R.F.A.

Army Form C. 2118.

XXXVI

Vol 6

INTELLIGENCE SUMMARY

(Erase heading not required.)

Place	Date	Hour	Summary of Events and Information	Remarks and references to Appendices
ENGLE-BELMER	1.4.16		165 Bde R.F.A. (31 Division) began to take over gun positions from 1st Brigade a section at a time.	
	2.4.16		Taking over complete and Brigade handed over charge at 11 am. Position of guns etc then became as follows.	
			"A" Battery in action near ENGLEBELMER (under command of O.C. Centre Group 36 Div. Arty)	
			"B" Battery 2 guns in action at AUCHONVILLERS (under command of "A" Battery) 2 guns at ACHEUX.	
			"C" guns at HEDAUVILLE. "D" Guns at HARPONVILLE. Ammunition columns at HEDAUVILLE.	
			NOTE. Guns had been exchanged & gun positions not relieving batteries of 165 Bde. No left behind fillited & taken place working parties, one in ENGLEBELMER.	

Army Form C. 2118.

WAR DIARY
or
INTELLIGENCE SUMMARY.
(Erase heading not required.)

Place	Date	Hour	Summary of Events and Information	Remarks and references to Appendices
ENGLE-BELMER	APRIL		Gun parties to be employed in preparing new Gun Position at Sedech place near ENGLEBELMER. Horses and remainder of the Bn. moved out of the line to ACHEUX, HEDAUVILLE and HOPPINVILLE.	
	12th		Lt. Col. P. WHEATLEY on transfer to R.H.A. handed over command of Brigade to Major A.D. MURRAY.	
	19th		C/173 moved into action in new position in MESNIL VALLEY, night	18/19 April
	20th		D/173 — do —	19/20 April
			Left group formed by A.B.C. D 1173 and B/154 to cover HAMEL SECTOR.	
			Bde H.Q. moved to MARTINSART.	
	26th		Major H.C. Simpson R.F.A. took over Command of the Brigade.	
MARTINSART	29/30	11.30 p.m	A/173 (and B/154, the How battery of left Group) took part in a bombardment lasting from 11.8's p.m to 12.35 am in support of a raid carried out by 29th Division. Rounds fired A/173. 360 H.E. shrapnel, 120 H.E. B/154. 272 H.E. Rounds fired 1839. H.E. 378.	
	1-30		Casualties during the month — Horses – Mules 1 killed 1 wounded.	

J.H.P.
Major R.F.A.
Commanding 173rd Bde R.F.A.

Off% A. G's Office   <u>SECRET.</u>
   The Base.

War Diary of the Brigade
under my command, for
month ending 31st May 1916
is forwarded herewith in
accordance with Field Service
Regulations, Part II, Sec 140

                H.C. Patton
                       Lieut Col
2/6/16   Comdg 173rd BdeRFA.

WAR DIARY
173rd Bde. R.F.A.
INTELLIGENCE SUMMARY

Army Form C. 2118.

(Erase heading not required.)

Place	Date	Hour	Summary of Events and Information	Remarks and references to Appendices
Martinsart	MAY 1.		Locations of Units. Bde HQrs. MARTINSART. 'A' Battery — ENGELBELMER. WAGON LINE. ENGELBELMER WOOD. B — AUCHONVILLERS — FORCEVILLE. C — MESNIL VALLEY — HEDAUVILLE. D — — — FORCEVILLE. Bde Am. Col. HEDAUVILLE.	
	7		36th Division carried out a raid on enemy lines. Centre bombardment was carried out by left group. 36th Div Arty, comprising 173rd Bde R.F.A. and B/152 (How) Bde. Bombardment, which was a feint, commenced at 11.58 p.m. "Cease fire" ordered at 12.38 am 8th. Telephone communication was satisfactory, but his to 'B' Battery was cut by shell fire. No casualties in the Brigade. No of rounds fired. A 173. 231 Shrapnel. 194 H.E. B 173, 274 Shrapnel. 26 H.E. C 173. 248 Shrapnel. D 173, 240 Shrapnel. 31 H.E. 20 H.E.	
	8-15		Nothing unusual to report. Ordinary trench warfare.	
	16	12.30 am	A heavy bombardment of its left (N) of our division front commenced. Infantry called for Artillery support as they anticipated an attack. All batteries in the front opened fire and, if any enemy attack was intended, it was stopped. After about two an hour the enemy fire on our front had almost ceased, the centre of disturbance having moved further N. on to the front of the 48th Division.	

WAR DIARY or INTELLIGENCE SUMMARY

Army Form C. 2118.

Place	Date	Hour	Summary of Events and Information	Remarks and references to Appendices
MARTIN	16.		The bombardment lasted about an hour. Casualties. One man wounded by shell fire. No of rounds fired. A173.190. B143.75. C173.114. D173.235.	
	17-20		Whole scheme of reorganization of Divisional Artillery, the Brigade Amm. Col. was disbanded. Together N.C.O.s and men posted to the D.A.C. 18 N.C.Os and men posted to Trench Mortars. Remainder distributed by Army posted to help up Battery establishments.	
	18/19		"A" Battery moved from ENGLEBELMER to new position in the HESNIL VALLEY. (Q21 a 4.8.) Detailed section of B/173 was moved from position in AUCHONVILLERS, to new position 300x S.W. of AUCHONVILLERS (Q8a 10.05)	
	20		Enemy shelled the position vacated by "A" Battery on the previous day, shelling was continuous throughout the afternoon, & was carried on again late at night.	
	21,22		Quiet day on our front – only usual desultory shelling on both sides.	
	23.		Quiet on our front. A bombardment of the Division on our left (29th Div.) commenced at 10.20 hrs and lasted half an hour. They did not require any assistance from us.	

WAR DIARY or INTELLIGENCE SUMMARY

Army Form C. 2118.

Place	Date	Hour	Summary of Events and Information	Remarks and references to Appendices
MARTINSART & MESNIL	MAY 24		Quiet day. "A" Battery wagon lines moved from ENGLEBELMER WOOD to HEDAUVILLE.	
	25,26,27 28,29,30,31		Quiet days – Only the normal operations of trench warfare. Total number of rounds fired during month 2534 shrapnel, 765 H.E. Casualties during month – two men – slightly wounded by shrapnel. During the month work was continued on all sense in construction and completion of battery positions. Reorganization of Brigade. In addition to abolition of Bde Am Col a further reorganization was carried into effect by which the composition of the Brigade was altered to 3 – 18 pr. batteries and one 4.5" How battery. "B" Battery 154 H (How) Bde being transferred to 173rd Bde and taking the designation of D/173. The original D/173 (18 pr battery) was transferred to 154 Bde under the title of B/154. D/173 (How) commanded by Major C.H. Scott, is in action in AVELUY WOOD. (9.34.C. 77th Map S7D S.E. 1/2-0000)	

H.C. Potter
Commdg 173 (W) Bde R.F.A.

Head Qtrs.

36th Divisional Artillery.

173rd BRIGADE.

ROYAL FIELD ARTILLERY.

JUNE 1916

C/427/73

Officer i/c D.A.G's Office
The Base.

H.Q. R.A., 36th Div having reported that War Diary for June had not reached your Office, a copy is forwarded herewith. Please acknowledge receipt.

W Burges L.

14/7/16   Adjt 173rd Bde R.F.A.

Army Form C. 2118.

WAR DIARY
INTELLIGENCE SUMMARY
(Erase heading not required.)

COPY

Place: MARTINSART

Date	Hour	Summary of Events and Information	Remarks and references to Appendices
JUNE 1-6		Quiet days. Hostile artillery north of trench envipair. Work on new positions in MESNIL VALLEY continued.	
6		On the night of 6/7 a raid was made by our Infantry on the enemy front line trenches at Q.18.c. (5.7.D.S.G./1/10000 - BEAUMONT). Bombardment commenced at 11.45 p.m. Raid was successful, infantry entering trenches at 12.20 a.m. and bombing several dug-outs and a tunnel containing electrical apparatus. No prisoners were taken.	
7.8.9.		Normal. Quiet days. Nothing to report.	
10/11		On the night of 10/11 the enemy artillery opened a heavy fire on our front line, communication and support trenches, at 11.30 p.m. At 11.35 p.m. the "S.O.S." call was received from Infantry and all batteries opened fire on their barrage. Hostile fire was heavier on the left of our front than on other parts from 11.47 p.m. till 12.15 a.m. when it began to slacken. Hostile fire continued to slacken until 12.30 a.m. when Infantry reported all quiet, and "cease fire" was ordered. Subsequent enquiry of parts of about 25 gold enemy attempted to	

WAR DIARY
INTELLIGENCE SUMMARY

Army Form C. 2118.
№ 12.

Place	Date	Hour	Summary of Events and Information	Remarks and references to Appendices
MARTINSART	JUNE 10/11		enter our trenches in the neighbourhood of WILLIAM REDAN (Q24a). They were met by heavy rifle & machine gun fire, and thus together with our artillery fire stopped the raid, only 5 of the enemy succeeding in getting into our line, and these were immediately bombed out.	
	12-18		Quiet days, during which nothing worthy of special notice occurred. Enemy artillery quiet. Three batteries No 44, 45, 74 & of 20th Regiment of Artillery (French) came into the area and occupied positions behind MESNIL (Q.27). Owing to the short time available, a large working party was provided from the Bde to assist them in their digging and construction & their positions were sufficiently complete to enable them to get into action in 2 or 3 days from commencement of work.	
	19			
	20		C/154 Battery (Capt A. Bruce) moved into its new position on the Ridge N. of MESNIL (Q.22.b) and came under the orders of Lt Col Long, thus completing the Group for purpose of the "Lt Army Scheme". The Group (commanded by Lt Col H.C. Sumpson D.S.O. 173rd Bde R.F.A. consists of the following Batteries.	

2353 Wt. W2544/1454 700,000 5/15 D. D. & L. A.D.S.S./Forms/C. 2118.

Army Form C. 2118.

WAR DIARY or INTELLIGENCE SUMMARY.

(Erase heading not required.)

Instructions regarding War Diaries and Intelligence Summaries are contained in F.S. Regs., Part II. and the Staff Manual respectively. Title pages will be prepared in manuscript.

Place	Date	Hour	Summary of Events and Information	Remarks and references to Appendices
MARTINSART	JUNE 20	—	A/173. Capt L.A.L. Brownlow. B/173 — J. N. Littleton C/173 — Major G.R.O. Edwards. D/173 (How) " B.A.R. Scott B/154 Capt A. H. Burns O.S.O. C/154 " A. Smith. Nothing unusual to report. Normal artillery actions of trench warfare.	
	21-22		Group Headquarters move from MARTINSART to Battle Station in the MESNIL VALLEY (Q.28.a) No. of rounds fired by the Brigade during the period from 1st to 22nd June. 18 pr. G.S. - Shrapnel 3904. H.E. 785. 4.5" How - H.E. 717.	
MESNIL	23.			
	24	9am	Lst Army Attack on Enemy commenced. Four Batteries, viz: A/173, C/173, B/152 & C/154 commenced wire-cutting, &c. was continued throughout the day. Gaps cut in front and support line were During night all Batteries bombarded communications in enemy lines & kept open gaps in wire. Casualties - Nil No. of rds. expended:— 18pr — Shrapnel 3670. H.E. 119. 4.5" — H.E. 148.	

WAR DIARY
INTELLIGENCE SUMMARY

Place: MESNIL

Date June	Hour	Summary of Events and Information	Remarks
25	a.m.	Wire cutting continued as on previous day by same batteries. Gaps cut in Support and Reserve line wire. The remaining 18 pr Battery (B/79) was employed in exploding enemy trenches. 9/VI and 9/18.C. also strayed communication trenches and shrapnel at intervals. 10/1/43 (How) bombarded various strong points, trench mortar & M.G. emplacements. Enemy artillery reply to our fire was practically negligible and no movement of or transport could be seen in or behind enemy lines. Casualties. Personnel — 1 slight, 3/refusal. Materiel — 1 pr, Shrapnel 4528. H.E. 1383. 4.5in How. H.E. 337. R.g. rounds fired. — Minor accidents — no guns out of action.	
26	M.	Wire cutting on three lines was continued as on previous days. Further gaps were cut, and those previously cut were widened. Fire was also kept up on communication trenches, and communication behind the front line. At night gaps in wire were kept open and communications sprinkled with shrapnel. Hostile Artillery not unusually active on our front, but there were heavy	

Army Form C. 2118.

WAR DIARY
INTELLIGENCE SUMMARY.
(Erase heading not required.)

Place	Date	Hour	Summary of Events and Information	Remarks and references to Appendices
MESNIL	JUNE 26.		Bombardments of our trenches in THIEPVAL WOOD during the day and night. Casualties Personnel Nil Matériel 3 guns out of action from enemy shells running out springs. Ammunition expended 18/h – 35578 shrapnel. 931 HE. 1st 449 HE.	
	27	X day	Were cutting, and widening of existing gaps was continued, also intermittent fire upon communication trenches and communications generally. Stokes bomb junctions of trenches, trench mortar and machine gun emplacements bombarded 9 & 5 Howitzers. During the night the Infantry made a successful raid on the enemy trenches. Enemy fired numerous rounds at different parts of the area around HAMEL and MESNIL at intervals during the day & night. A few lachrymatory shell were fired, which caused some inconvenience but no serious effect.	

Army Form C. 2118.

WAR DIARY
INTELLIGENCE SUMMARY.
(Erase heading not required.)

Place	Date	Hour	Summary of Events and Information	Remarks and references to Appendices
MESNIL	JUNE 28		Bombardment of enemy trenches and communications continued. Gaps in wire still further widened. Enemy artillery more active than during previous day, & there are indications that some fresh batteries are being moved up, although the heavy guns appear to have been withdrawn. Night tasks, as on previous nights — keeping gaps in wire open and clear.	
	29			
	30		Owing to heavy state of ground on account of much rain, the assault did not take place on 29th as originally arranged. Two further days were allotted to preliminary bombardment, and during this period no message of particular importance received.	

Y. & Z. days.   Y.1. Day.

Lt. H.C. Simpson Kimber
for adj. 173rd Bde. R.F.A.

36th Divisional Artillery.

173rd BRIGADE.

ROYAL FIELD ARTILLERY.

JULY 1916

Army Form C. 2118.

WAR DIARY
INTELLIGENCE SUMMARY.
(Erase heading not required.)

173rd BRIGADE R.F.A.

Instructions regarding War Diaries and Intelligence Summaries are contained in F. S. Regs., Part II. and the Staff Manual respectively. Title pages will be prepared in manuscript.

Place	Date	Hour	Summary of Events and Information	Remarks and references to Appendices
MESNIL VALLEY	JULY 1 "Z" day.	6.25 am	Preliminary Bombardment finished. Intensive Bombardment of enemys lines prior to launching of the attack. Bombardment lasted from 6.25 am till 7.30 am. At 7.30 am Infantry attack launched & artillery fire lifted to Reserve or "B" line trenches.	
			Attack by 7.36th Division suffered very heavy casualties, and were unable to exceed the present sky. Red fused on their flanks were in the air, rung by 32nd Div on right and 29th Div on left being held up, chiefly by machine guns.	
		10.30 am	Enemy reported to be massing in trenches in R.24. for counter attack. A barrage was at once put on and attack did not materialize. By 5 pm. the were practically brought could be seen retiring over R.14 and R.19.	
		1 pm	Our Infantry could be seen retiring over R.14 and R.19. By 7 pm the were back on their own lines except for a small force which returned to held in enemy front line & Support trenches in R.19c.	
			At night of 26/1/ 31st Div Infantry were relieved by 49th Div. and the remnants of 36th Div were relieved, withdrawn.	
			The 3rd Div Arty remained in their positions and came under orders of 49 th Div.	
			Casualties – Nil Ammn expended by Group. 56.0 A. 2900 AX. 1500 BX.	
	2,3,4 & 5.		Bombardment general day. – almost approaching the condition of ordinary trench warfare. Fire was maintained continuously on enemy trenches and strong points during the day and on all communications by night.	

WAR DIARY
INTELLIGENCE SUMMARY.

Army Form C.2118.

173rd BRIGADE — R.F.A.

Place	Date	Hour	Summary of Events and Information	Remarks and references to Appendices
MESNIL	JULY 2,3,4 & 5		Enemy artillery fairly quiet until 2nd and 5th when a considerable number of 105mm and 77mm shells were fired along MESNIL Ridge and along the Valley. A material damage was done. One man in B/154 was wounded slightly when bringing up ammunition. Some 150mm shells were also fired into MESNIL and the tramway lined (Jacobs Ladder) between MESNIL and HAMEL. On these days a considerable number of lachrymatory shell were fired into AVELUY WOOD. On the night of 5th the Group was withdrawn from action in the MESNIL Valley, and marched to AVELUY and relieved the 6th Group of the 19th Divl Artillery, coming under command of C.R.A. 12th Division. Group HQ were at W18c7.8, A Battery at W9a22, C Battery at W12d2.6 and D Battery at W18c7.3. B/143 and C/154 attached to Right Group and B/154 to Left Group. Wagon lines of all units on the ALBERT-MILLENCOURT Road - B2 Central.	
AVELUY	6.		Nothing special to report.	

Army Form C. 2118.

WAR DIARY
INTELLIGENCE SUMMARY.
(Erase heading not required.)

73rd BRIGADE R.F.A.

Place	Date	Hour	Summary of Events and Information	Remarks and references to Appendices
AVELUY	JULY 7		Bombardment of Eastern part of the Village of OVILLERS and the trenches South and East of the village by Field and Heavy Artillery continued with a few Barrages of French Artillery, commencing at 4.30 am. Intermittent bursts till 8.35 am.	
	8		Bombardment of OVILLERS and trenches South & East of in support of Infantry attack on trench X14 b 75 - X 18 a 1.8.	
	9,10,11		Several artillery operations against OVILLERS and trenches South and East, and North-East as far as POZIERES.	
	12		R/d Sub-Sect relieved by 25 D.A. Coy.	
	13		On nght of 13/14 all artillery belongs to 36 C.D. Withdrawn from action and return to their engine-lines. Group System suspended and units revert to Nothing to report. Brigade-organisation.	
	14		Bgde marched N, via DOULLENS and billeted night of 14th at LE MARAIS SEC and MILLY.	
	15		Continued march via GROUCHES - BOUQUEMAISON and BUNNIERES and billeted at MONCHY.	

2353 Wt. W2544/1454 700,000 5/15 D.D.&L. A.D.S.S./Forms/C. 2118.

WAR DIARY

INTELLIGENCE SUMMARY.
(Erase heading not required.)

Army Form C. 2118.

Place	Date	Hour	Summary of Events and Information	Remarks and references to Appendices
	JULY 16		Marched via FLERS – CROISETTE – WAVRANS & billets at MONCHY.	
	17		Marched via FONTAINE – FEBVIN PALFART – FLECHIN and ENGUINEGATTE to THEROUANNE (billet)	
	18		Marched via BLENDECQUES – ST OMER – TILQUES and NORDAUSQUES to RECQUES and POLINCOVE, this being the billeting area selected for rest and refitting. Bde HQ and 'B' Battery at RECQUES, 'A' at MUNQ NIERLET, 'C' at POLINCOVE and 'D' at MUNQ NIERLET.	
	19 20		Received orders to relieve 24th Div Art.	
	21		Marched via ST MARTIN AU LAERT and ARQUES to billets at WALLON CAPPEL.	
	22		Marched via HAZEBROUCK and STRAZEELE to billets at MOOLENACKER (METEREN)	
			Marched via METEREN and BAILLEUL to DRANOUTRE on the Belgian Front. Relieved the 108th FAB Group, and came into action for 50th Div. Artillery.	

WAR DIARY or INTELLIGENCE SUMMARY

Army Form C. 2118.

Place	Date	Hour	Summary of Events and Information	Remarks and references to Appendices
	JULY			
	22		Took over as left Group, and the following batteries, A, B, C & D/173, B/251 and one section of B/154. Group H/Qrs at DRANOUTRE. Batteries in action in front of KEMMEL HILL. Wagon lines near DRANOUTRE. Group covering 151st Infantry Brigade.	
	23, 24		Enemy artillery considerable activity with trench mortars and Minniewerfen.	
	25, 26		Very quiet day — usual operations of trench warfare.	
	27		D/173 relieved by D/251, and section B/154 by C/251. D/173 and B/154 move to command of Right Group. A/173 passed to command of Centre Group.	
	29		Group HQ move to LITTLE KEMMEL	
	30		Group taken over by 251st Bde, 50th Div. Group HQ move to T.21.c.27. — S. of NEUVE EGLISE.	
	31		A/173 & C/173 withdrawn from action and retire to wagon lines. B/173 & relieved by B/253 and relieves C/183.	

HCE

Hdq E.C.
Cmdg 173rd Bde R.F.A.

Army Form C. 2118.

173 Bde

WAR DIARY
or
INTELLIGENCE SUMMARY.
(Erase heading not required.)

Instructions regarding War Diaries and Intelligence Summaries are contained in F.S. Regs., Part II. and the Staff Manual respectively. Title pages will be prepared in manuscript.

Place	Date	Hour	Summary of Events and Information	Remarks and references to Appendices
NEUVE EGLISE HILL 63	August 1.		One Section A/173 withdrawn from action to wagon line " " C/173 withdrawn and moved into new position at T.23.a.7.3.	Reference Maps — France & Belgium 27 SW. 1/ 28 NW. 1/
	2		Remaining Section of A/173 withdrawn, and Battery occupied new position at T.23.f.4.6. Only 2 emplacements completed — 2 guns in action, 2 at wagon line. Remaining Section of C/173 withdrawn from old position. Only 3 emplacements ready in new position, one gun put in action, making total of 3, and one at wagon line. All Batteries in Brigade changed wagon lines to new positions as under — A/173 S.24.d.3.2 B/173 k B.2.c.8.6. C/173 k B.2.c.8.3 and D/173 G B.3.c.5.5.	
	3, 4, 5.		Very quiet days — nothing to report.	
	6		No operations to report Re-arrangement of Groups of 36th Div'l Art'y. 173rd Bde + B/154 forming the Right Group under Lieut. Col. H.C. Simpson D.S.O. Battery positions as follows :—	
			A/173 T.23.d.4.6. B/173 T.24.a.1.9 C/173 T.23.a.7.3 D/173 T.24 d 9.4 B/154 T.17 d 3.2	

Army Form C. 2118.

23.

WAR DIARY
INTELLIGENCE SUMMARY

Place	Date	Hour	Summary of Events and Information	Remarks and references to Appendices
NEUVE EGLISE HILL 63	August 7,8,9 10,11,12,13		Very quiet days. Hostile fire practically nil, except for a certain amount of Trench Mortar activity against our front line trenches. General from 4 p.m. to 6 p.m.	All map references Fleurbaix France & Belgium, 28 S.W. & 36 N.W.
	14		On night of 14/15 the Divisional front was extended to about the left up to N.36.a.5.1. the right, from U.14.b.9.5. to U.8.a.3.2., being held by 10 gd Infantry Bde, and covered by Right Group (143/184) R.F.A., the portion of enemy front line so covered being from U.5.a.2.9 to U.8.a.9.5. the batteries from right to left being B/173. B/154. A/173. C/173.	
	15		On night of 10/11th the renowned gun of C/173 was brought into action at T.23.a.7.3. No operations, other than that of normal trench warfare. Wagon lines moved to new positions as under:— A/173 to T.19.b.b.4. B/173 to S.29.b.9.1. and C/173 to S.29.2.9.4. One section of B/154 came out of action and made retired to Wagon Line.	
	16		Hostile artillery displayed rather more activity than of late. C/153 was shelled with 105 mm H.E. for 3/4 hour (4 p.m. – 4.45 p.m.) During afternoon roads in vicinity of PETIT DOUVE and PETITE MUNQUE were sprayed with shrapnel. Remaining section of B/154 came out of action, and the left section of A/173 went	

Army Form C. 2118.

WAR DIARY
or
INTELLIGENCE SUMMARY.
(Erase heading not required)

Instructions regarding War Diaries and Intelligence Summaries are contained in F. S. Regs., Part II and the Staff Manual respectively. Title pages will be prepared in manuscript.

24.

All map references 1/20,000 BELGIUM & FRANCE 28 S.W. 31 N.W.

Place	Date	Hour	Summary of Events and Information	Remarks and references to Appendices
NEUVE EGLISE HILL 63.	August 16		went into action. Right group again reconstructed, and now consists of the four Batteries of 173rd Bde only, in action at positions already indicated.	
	17		Operations Nothing to report. Map ref of B, C and A Batteries moved to new positions as under:— A/173. T.19.b.4.6. B/173. S.29.b.9.2. C/173. S.29.b.9.3.	
	18		Nothing to report.	
	19		Nothing to report. Very quiet	
	20		Operations - Normal trench warfare D/173 compy hive moved to B.8.b.0.7.	
	21,22,23		} Quiet days Usual operations of trench warfare	
	24,25			
	26		Operations Nil. C/173 moved from T.23.a.7.3. to position recently occupied by B/173 at T.17.d.4.3.	

T:134. Wt. W708-776. 510000. 4/15. Sir J. C. & S.

Army Form C. 2118.

WAR DIARY
INTELLIGENCE SUMMARY.
(Erase heading not required.)

Place: NEUVE EGLISE / HILL 63

Date	Hour	Summary of Events and Information	Remarks and references to Appendices
August 27		Quiet day. Nothing to report. Battery wagon lines were moved, as under, owing to a rearrangement of Divisional areas:— B/173 } C/173 } to S.24.b.3.2 D/173 to T.20.c.1.9	Reference to map 27 S.W. 1/20000
28		Quiet day. Nothing unusual to report. Weather wet, and misty and S-westerly wind.	
29/30		Hostile Artillery quiet. Our 18 pr batteries carried out a certain amount of wire cutting at points on enemy front line wire in preparation for a raid following a fast attack, to be delivered when wind is favourable.	
31	1.30 am	Weather being favourable, gas was emitted from the front of 109th Inf^y Bde. (Trenches 128, 129 & 130) at full denity for fifteen minutes.	
	1.34 am to 2.4 am	Bombardment of enemy front line and support trenches by 18 pr^s and 4.5 in Howitzers. The "Gas barrage" was not called for by Infantry. From 1 & 5 am kill 3 am the enemy made a feeble retaliation.	See appendix "A"

Army Form C. 2118.

26

WAR DIARY
INTELLIGENCE SUMMARY
(Erase heading not required.)

Place	Date	Hour	Summary of Events and Information	Remarks and references to Appendices
NEUVE EGLISE and HILL 63	August 31		During the day enemy fired a fair amount of 105 mm ammunition over the area immediately west of, and on the western & south western slopes of HILL 63. Fire was heaviest between 2 p.m. and 4 p.m. During this time a direct hit was obtained on the telephone dug out of A/173 and two men in C/173 received slight wounds from splinters of steel. This was, apparently, retaliation for the bombardment of the early morning. Total number of rounds fired during the month :— 4.2" = A. 719 A.X. 608 B.X. Casualties - none except those referred to above on 31st. During the month all hands were occupied in completing the positions taken over, and strengthening them to make them proper against shell up to 150 mm, and the 18 pr. batteries commenced enlarging their positions to take 6 guns each. Work also started on horse standings and winter accommodation generally.	

H.C. Ruff
Comdg 143rd Bde R.F.A. Kent to L

Appendix "A"

1. In accordance with instructions, a Gas Attack will be delivered tonight if the wind is favourable.
2. The time the gas will be emitted is 1.30 a.m.
3. The attack will consist of –
   (a) A discharge of gas at full density for 15 minutes
   (b) A bombardment of the enemy's front line and support trenches, beginning at 1.34 a.m. and ending at 2.4 a.m.
   (c) A strong patrol will go out with the object of entering the enemy's line and obtaining identification, etc.,
4. Corps Artillery is co-operating.
5. If the weather is favourable, a message confirming the attack will be sent shortly after 10 p.m. Should the wind be unfavourable after this a message will be sent, cancelling the attack. This message will be "THE ANSWER IS NOW NO".
6. No mention of these operations will be made over the telephone at any time.
7. From 9.30 p.m., all telephone lines will be reserved for tactical purposes.
8. The bombardment will be carried out by Right Group, as per Appendix A.
9. After the raid is over the Right Group may be called upon for a barrage to assist the infantry to return from the hostile trenches. This barrage will be put on as per App: B. The signal for this barrage will be three pairs of red Very lights, sent up in succession at the point of entry, i.e. U9c 23.00. This signal will be reported by the Officer in charge of rocket picquet, who will give the order "BARRAGE" to all Batteries of the Group. The signal for the barrage will also be sent

by telephone through Battalion HQrs, and the Liaison Officer will telephone the word "BARRAGE" to all Batteries.

10.
During the raid, which leaves our trenches at 2.30 a.m., B/173 will fire at a rate of one round per minute at the Sap running from U15a 30.80 to U15a 4 98.80 being very careful not to go north of this at any time

D/173 will fire one round every two minutes at AVENUE FARM and Farm at U15b 2.8.

Sd/. H.C. Simpson Lt.Col.
Comdg Right Group

Appendix A.

Batteries will bombard their own part of the front line and the second line immediately in rear of it, searching and sweeping to cover all the ground.

The rate of fire will be :—

18 pdr — 1.34 — 1.40. Section fire 10 secs
         1.40 — 2.2   "   "   15 "
         2.2 — 2.4   "   "   5 "

Howitzers will fire Section fire 20 secs throughout, on their own places for defence, except that the two southern guns will fire on the barricade at U.15.a.3.8 instead of their normal places.

Appendix B.

A/173 will barrage front line U9c 05.50 — U8b 60.00
C/173 "   "   from U9c 65.55 — U15a 70.90
B/173 "   "   "   U15a 70.90 — U15a 30.80 with three guns, and fire along sap U15a 30.80 — U14b 98.80 with remaining gun.

A battery of Centre Group will barrage from
        U9c 05.50 — U9c 65.55

D/173 will fire as follows :—

    1 gun on   U9c 05.50
    1 "   "   U9c 80.05
    1 "   "   U15a 70.90
    1 "   "   U15a 30.80

Rate of fire. Section fire 15 secs.

Infantry will order 'Cease fire'.

Vol II

Confidential.

War Diary
of
173rd Bde R.F.A.

Period 1st to 30th September 1916.

Vol. I.

Army Form C. 2118.

27.

WAR DIARY
INTELLIGENCE SUMMARY.

(Erase heading not required.)

Place	Date	Hour	Summary of Events and Information	Remarks and references to Appendices
NEUVE EGLISE and HILL 63.	SEPTEMBER 1.	1.30 am	Bombardment of enemy front line in support of Gas attack by 107th and 108th Infantry Bdes (Centre & left Bdes of 36 Div). Programme same as for bombardment 12th am to 2-4 am on morning of 31/7/16 (q.v.) Enemy retaliation slight on our front line. Remainder of day quiet.	Ref reference to Sheet 28 SW 1/20000
	2.		Quiet during the day.	
		10.30 pm	Order "GAS ALERT" received. Shortly after, at 10.40 pm, 69th Bde, 23rd Div. gave "GAS ALARM". All batteries warned and immediately opened fire, putting a slow barrage on NO MANS LAND. At 11.10 pm rate of fire reduced to ½ original rate. 11.40 pm. information received that this was false alarm and "Cease firing" ordered.	
	3, 4, 45.		Quiet days. Normal trench warfare. 2 Lieut A. Willcox D/173 evacuated to England - sick —— N.T. Simpkin B/173 " "	
	6.		Hostile Artillery quiet. During the afternoon a bombardment commencing at 3pm, of a portion of the enemy line in N.36.d was carried out. Programme and time table attached. No other areas were issued. Enemy retaliation nil.	Appx "A"

Army Form C. 2118.

27A

WAR DIARY
INTELLIGENCE SUMMARY.
(Erase heading not required)

Instructions regarding War Diaries and Intelligence Summaries are contained in F. S. Regs., Part II and the Staff Manual respectively. Title pages will be prepared in manuscript.

Place	Date	Hour	Summary of Events and Information	Remarks and references to Appendices
	SEPTEMBER			
	6		Information was received that the enemy were to carry out a relief on a large scale during 6th and following days and arrangements were made for a bombardment of his front and support lines, communication etc. For this purpose the following programme was drawn up —	
			A/173 .. 2 guns on communication trench from U9c 00.90 to U10a 00.60.	
			" " " — U9c 00.88 to U10a 28.13	
			B/173 " " — U9c 45.05 to U10a 45.65	
			C/173 " " — U8b 40.40 to U9a 70.90	
			D/173 1 gun on each of the following points :— U8b 5.5, U9a 1.5	
			U9c 4.1 and U15a 3.9.	
			In addition to the above occasional bursts were fired on suspected assembly places at GREY FARM (U9a 79) & A/173, LA POTTERIE FARM (U10a9) by B/173 and SCHNITZEL FARM (U3c 8.3)	
			An intermittent bombardment was maintained on these points from 12 noon 6/9/16 till 10 a.m. 8/9/16.	

T.134. Wt. W708-776. 500000. 4/15. Sir J. C. & S.

WAR DIARY or INTELLIGENCE SUMMARY

Army Form C. 2118.

28.

Place: NEUVE EGLISE & HILL 63

Date	Hour	Summary of Events and Information	Remarks and references to Appendices

SEPTEMBER

7. Rearrangement of Divisional Front was completed, the 19th Division taking over the N half of the line previously held by the Right Brigade of 36th Div. ie the part of front covered by this Group.
Operations - Very quiet day. Nothing to report.

8. 10am. Right Group 36th Div Arty (173rd Bde) passed to tactical command of 23rd Divr. 'B' Group left Group 23rd Div Arty.
Operations. Nil.
Reliefs. D/173 and D/76 relieved each other, the latter unit coming temporarily for tactical purpose under command of this Group.
D/173 moved to new Battery position at N.27 a 1.3, with origin lid at N.28 d.1.7., and passed temporarily to left Group 36th D.A.
Operations. Nil. Horse Artillery very quiet.

9. Command Group passed to command of 19th Divl Arty who relieved 23rd Divl Arty at 6 pm.
Reliefs. Personnel of one section each of B and C Batteries, 173rd Bde relieved by A and B Batteries 86 Bde R.F.A. respectively. The latter two

Map Reference to Sheet 28 S.W. 1/20000

WAR DIARY
INTELLIGENCE SUMMARY

Army Form C. 2118.

29.

Place	Date	Hour	Summary of Events and Information	Remarks and references to Appendices
NEUVE EGLISE	SEPTEMBER			
	9		Batteries having been reorganised on 6 gun establishment, sent up one section personnel and one section complete with guns. Personnel of C/143 moved to wagon line at M34 d 1.7 and took over guns from C/154. B/143 to wagon line at M33 a 1.7, and took over guns from B/154. A/143 and C/142 relieved each other personnel only. A/143 going into action at N 33 a 8.1. and having to command of Left Group, 36 D.A. A/143 wagon line remained at T 19 d 4.6. Operations Nil. Very quiet day.	Not returns of 9.S.M. 1/5000.
	10		Reliefs. Relieving sections of "B" and "C" Batteries relieved by corresponding sections (personnel only in each case) of A and B, 76th Bde. and joined their older sections at important sections at important Operations Nil very quiet.	
	11		O.C. 143 Bde relinquished command of Left Group 19th Div., handing over the front to OC 86thBde, and assuming command of Left Group 36th Divl Artillery. Bde Headquarters moving to DRANOUTRE (M35 d 9.4)	

WAR DIARY
INTELLIGENCE SUMMARY.
(Erase heading not required.)

Army Form C. 2118.

Instructions regarding War Diaries and Intelligence Summaries are contained in F.S. Regs., Part II. and the Staff Manual respectively. Title pages will be prepared in manuscript.

Place	Date	Hour	Summary of Events and Information	Remarks and references to Appendices
DRANOUTRE	SEPTEMBER 11		Operations. Very quiet. Nothing to report. Reorganization of this Brigade to form three 6-gun 18 pr Batteries and one 4-gun 4.5 inch How. Battery commenced. A/173 and C/173 made up to 6-gun establishment by the posting of one section of B/173 to each vag. – Left section to B/173 and Right Section to C/173. This was completed by 12 midnight 11/9/16. The Group Hdqrs consisted of three 6-gun batteries, A/173 – B/173, C/173 and B/154 and one Howitzer Battery – D/173.	Map reference to Ypres Sheet 28 S.W.
	12, 13.		Operations. Nil. Ordinary trench warfare. Very quiet days.	
	14		Operations. Nil. Very quiet. Reorganization B/154 Battery R.F.A. – a complete six-gun battery joined with the whole of its personnel, horses and equipment, to B/173, thus completing the Brigade up to the new establishment. Moves. All Battery wagon lines moved to new locations as under:– A/173 to M.34.d.3.8. B/173 to S.5.b.8.2. C/173 to S.5.b.8.3. D/173 to S.5.a.5.5.	

Army Form C. 2118.

WAR DIARY
INTELLIGENCE SUMMARY.
(Erase heading not required)

Instructions regarding War Diaries and Intelligence Summaries are contained in F.S. Regs., Part II. and the Staff Manual respectively. Title pages will be prepared in manuscript.

3/-

Place	Date	Hour	Summary of Events and Information	Remarks and references to Appendices
DRANOUTRE	SEPTEMBER 15		Operations. Very quiet. Reorganisation. Details (personnel, horses and equipment) from the late B/143 Battery posted to 36th D.A.C. thus completing the change. Billings officers Lieut. B.H.B. Allen B/143 posted to R.H.A. 2nd Indian Cavalry Division. On completion of reorganisation the Officers of the Brigade were as follows. A Battery. Lt.Col. H.C. Sampson D.S.O. Comdg. Bde. Capt. 6.A.L. Brandon Comdg. Lieut. W. Burges R.G.A. Adjt. Lieut. J.C. Dunkley Lieut. A.J. Gimson R.F.A. Orderly Officer. 2nd Lieut. J.S.A. Hunt " R.P. Schroeder " D.M. Bielawska " J. Butchel	

Army Form C. 2118.
32

WAR DIARY
of
INTELLIGENCE SUMMARY.

Place	Date	Hour	Summary of Events and Information	Remarks and references to Appendices
	SEPTEMBER		Officers (cont.)	
	15		"B" Battery	
			Capt. A.H. Burne & 2nd Comdg.	
			Lieut. A.R.G. Guinness	
			" E.J. Jackson	
			2nd Lieut. R.M. Hamman	
			" E. Yorke	
			" W.E. Steele	
			"C" Battery	
			Major G.R.O. Edwards Comdg.	
			Capt. J.N. Littleton	
			Lieut. A. Bowie	
			2nd Lieut. H.H. Achilles	
			" K.R. Pickett	
			" A.H. Angel	
			"D" Battery	
			Major C.A.R. Scott Comdg.	
			Lieut. G.A. Pickins	
			" P.J. Flanagan	
			" J.J. Kennedy	
			Lieut. E.J. Orr	
			" J.L. Hardie	
			Capt. J.R. Cockcroft (Veterinary)	
			Attached	
			Capt. J.A. McBlutock A.V.C.	
			" R.G. Blair R.A.M.C.	

WAR DIARY / INTELLIGENCE SUMMARY

Army Form C. 2118.

Place	Date	Hour	Summary of Events and Information	Remarks and references to Appendices
	SEPTEMBER			
	16		**Operations.** During the night 15th/16th a bombardment of enemy's line, communication trenches and strong points was carried out, in accordance with attached programme. The total number of rounds fired by our troops for this purpose was 795 A, 322 A.X. and 132 B.X. Enemy retaliation was very feeble, practically nil.	Appx "B"
	17		**Operations.** Enemy artillery very quiet, but hostile trench mortars were more active than usual against our trenches in N.36.v.	
		11.55 pm	"GAS" alarm was sent back by Infantry from our front line. Some rounds were fired in accordance with Defence Scheme instructions for delivery of a gas attack, but investigation proved the alarm also having been caused by a leakage from a gas cylinder in our own trenches.	
			Organization. Owing to re-organization of the Artillery, the existing system of administration of Trench Mortar Batteries was altered, the Batteries now being attached, for tactical purposes, to Groups	

Instructions regarding War Diaries and Intelligence Summaries are contained in F. S. Regs., Part II. and the Staff Manual respectively. Title pages will be prepared in manuscript.

WAR DIARY
~~or~~
~~INTELLIGENCE~~ SUMMARY.
(~~Erase heading not required.~~)

Army Form C. 2118.

34.

Place	Date	Hour	Summary of Events and Information	Remarks and references to Appendices
	SEPTEMBER			
	17		of the Divisional Artillery. Under this arrangement, the following Batteries were attached to Left Group (173rd Bde) with effect from 17/9/16 –	
			X.36 Medium Trench Mortar Battery. Lieut R.P. Prentys Comdg and	
			V.36 Heavy " " " Capt Powell "	
DRANOUTRE	18		Operations. Enemy artillery very quiet	
			The Infantry reported that early in the morning the enemy blew a mine in NO MANS LAND at N.36 d 05.90, and that work was going on in, and behind, the crater. A small bombardment was arranged to deal with this as shown on attached	App^x "C"
	19		Operations. Generally very quiet. During the morning a few medium trench mortar bombs fell in our lines ~~at~~ N24 a and d.	
	20		Operations. Hostile Artillery quiet, but Trench Mortars displayed considerable activity between 6.30 pm and 7 pm. Our Medium T.Ms replied effectively.	
	21. ~~22~~		Operations. Nil. Very quiet	
	22	3pm	Operations. A bombardment of enemy front line, lasting for an	

T.2134. Wt. W708–776. 500000. 4/15. Sir J. C. & S.

Army Form C. 2118.

WAR DIARY
or
INTELLIGENCE SUMMARY.
(Erase heading not required.)

Place	Date	Hour	Summary of Events and Information	Remarks and references to Appendices
DRANOUTRE	SEPTEMBER			
	22		Arty fr. heavy and medium trench mortars, and covering fire from T.M.s and M.Gs in towers was carried out in accordance with attached programme.	Apx "D"
	23		Very quiet.	
	24		Operations. Between 6 a.m and 7 a.m about 50 medium and heavy trench mortar and minenwerfer shots were fired on our trenches in N 36 a. Some damage was done to trenches and a few casualties among the Infantry were reported. Our trench mortars retaliated effectively. Remainder of day was quiet.	
	25, 26		Very quiet.	
	27		Operations. Nil. Enemy very quiet. Intelligence. An enemy observation balloon which had broken adrift (reported to have come from BAPAUME) was sighted about 5.45 p.m. It was chased by A.A. guns, and then attacked by our aeroplanes. It caught fire and eventually came down at N 31 f central. The observer, who was practically unhurt, was released from the wrecked car, and taken into custody	

Army Form C. 2118.

36.

WAR DIARY
INTELLIGENCE SUMMARY.
(Erase heading not required.)

Place	Date	Hour	Summary of Events and Information	Remarks and references to Appendices
	SEPTEMBER			
	28		Operations. A Bombardment of enemy's front line system, by 9.2, 18 Hows, 9.2 4.5" and Medium, Heavy & Light Trench Mortars was carried out in accordance with attached programme. Hostile retaliation very feeble.	Apps E.
	29		Very quiet - Nothing to report.	
	29/30		Operations. At 10 p.m. a raid on the enemy front line was carried out by 10th R. Innis Fus. A supporting barrage was put on by this Group as shown in Appendix "F". The infantry called for the barrage and our fire was opened at 10.40 p.m. and ceased, at order from infantry, at 11.23 p.m. The raid was successful, though 20 prisoners were taken. A machine gun was captured. Our casualties (infantry) two men wounded. Enemy retaliation very slight.	App=F.

W.C. Peel Lieut. Col.
Comdg 173rd Brigade R.F.A.

Appendix "A"

Secret

36th Divisional Artillery Order No 12.

A Bombardment for the destruction of a portion of the enemy's front line will be carried out on the 6th September, 1916, commencing at 4 p.m. in accordance with the attached Table.

Watches will be synchronized by telephone at 12 noon 6th instant.

The Bombardment will commence with one salvo from each Battery and will afterwards continue at a steady rate of fire till ammunition is expended.

L E Shaweck
Major R.A.
Brigade Major, 36th Divl. Artillery

4th September 1916.

Copy No 1. to R.A. 18th Corps
2. to 36th Divn "G"
3. to 153rd Bde R.F.A
4. to 154th Bde R.F.A
5. to 172nd Bde R.F.A
6. to 173rd Bde R.F.A
No 7. to 86th Bde R.F.A
8. to T.M.S.O.
9. to 107th Infy Bde
10. to 109th Infy Bde
11. to War Diary
12. to Filed
13. to H.A.G IX Corps

Appendix "E"

Reference Map 28 SWI 1/10000.

Copy No

Left Group Order No 2

27. 9. 16

1. There will be a bombardment of the enemy front line system by Left Group on Thursday 28th inst beginning at 9 a.m.

2. The following time table will be observed

    9.0 am — 9.15 am   Bombardment
    9.15 am — 9.35 am   Interval
    9.35 — 9.50   Bombardment
    9.50 — 10.10   Interval
    10.10 — 10.25   Bombardment

3. Watches will be synchronised at 8.30 a.m. O'C's X36 and Y36 (1 gun at R.E Yard) will receive correct time from Artillery Liaison Officer with Right Battalion at 8.15 a.m.

    Artillery Liaison Officer with Right Battalion will synchronise his watch with his battalion at 8 am

4. The targets engaged will be as follows:-

    1 Gun Y36 Heavy Trench Mortar Battery
        Support line N36a 88.53 - N36a 78.76.
    X36 Trench Mortar Battery (3 guns)
        Front line N36a 62.50 - N36a 55.80
    Stokes Mortars 109 Infy Bde
        Front line N36a 62.50 - N36a 55.80 .
    B/173 Front line N36a 65.45 - N36a 50.90
        and communication trenches between front and support line in this area.
    C/173 Support line N36a 98.45 - N30c 72.00
    D/173 Will block following points
        N36a 62.50   N36a 78.76   N36a 58.65
        - 55.80   - 88.53   - 80.70
    also Longear and cross roads N36a 25.85

Detached section of A/173 will fire during the
intervals on front and support lines as follows:

Front line   N36a 62.52 — N30c 54.15
Support line N36a 96.25 — N30c 72.00

Ammunition allowed:

French Mortar batteries as much as
possible in the time.

  A/173 (Detached Section)   80 rounds
  B/173   100
  C/173   100
  D/173   100

18 pdr to use 50% H.E.

Rates of fire to be worked out by Battery
Commanders to cover whole period of bombardment
except for detached section of A/173 which will
maintain a steady rate of fire during the intervals
of 1 round per gun per minute.

Trenches E1, D6, and D5 will be cleared.

Acknowledge.

Issued at 6 p.m.

Copies to:
1. 36th Div Arty
2. 109th Infy Bde
3. D.T.M.O.
4. A)
5. B) 173
6. C)
7. D)
8. X36 T.M. Bty
9. V36 H.T.M. Bty
10, 11. File

H Burgess
For Lieut Col
Commanding Left Group

Appendix 6

A/173 Front line   N36b 17.99 – N36b 15.00 – 80 rounds
B/173 Support line   N36d 25.90 – N36d 00.10 – 80 rounds
D/173 2 Guns on track N36d 05.90   – 20 rounds

2.30 p.m.

17.9.16

Appendix 6

Left Group
26th Divisional Artillery

1. Information has been received from the Infantry in the front line that the enemy fired a mine in No Mans Land at 6.30 this morning and that work is now going on in, and behind the crater.

2. A minor bombardment by Left Group, to deal with this will be carried out this afternoon in accordance with attached programme.

3. Battery Commanders will regulate rate of fire in order to cover from 3.30 p.m. to 4 p.m.

17.9.16

sd/- H.C. Simpson.
Lieut Col
Commanding Left Group
R.F.A.

Appendix "D"

Copy No 12
20.9.16
Ref 10000 sheet 28

Left Group Operation Order No:

1. A bombardment by Trench Mortars assisted by the Artillery of the Left group will take place on 22.9.16

2. Time of commencement of bombardment will be 3 p.m. and duration 1 hour

3. The following will take part in the bombardment

     2   2" T.M of X 36 Battery
     1   Heavy T.M. of X 36

     B/173
     C/173
     D/173

     Stokes Mortars belonging to 109 Infy Bde

4. The objective will be enemy front line trenches enclosed in following quadrilateral

     N 36 a 52.82 — N 30 c 50.28. N 30 c 68.15
     N 36 a 75.88

     The 2" T.M's will fire on the front line
     Heavy T.M. on Support line

     D/173 on following points   N 36 a 82.95
                                         N 30 c 53.05
                                         N 36 a 75.92
                                         N 30 c 72.05

     Stokes Mortars on front line

B/173 and C/173 will give covering fire on their own zone during the bombardment.

5. Ammunition allowed

    4.5" How.   40 rounds Bx
18 pdr. Batteries   25 rounds B & 25 rounds A x each
    2 T.M's   120 rounds
    Heavy T.M. as much as possible in time.

6. There will be a pause of 5 minutes at 3.30 p.m.

7. Trenches D6, E1 and E3 will be cleared

8. Acknowledge.

                          H Burgo
                          Lt R.F.A.
                   for Lt Col R.F.A.
                 Commanding Left Group

Copies to
1. 36th Divisional Artillery
2. 109th Infantry Bde.
3. ―――
4. V 36 T.M. Battery
5. X 36
6. A/173
7. B/173
8. C/173
9. D/173
10. T.M. S.C.
11, 12. File.

Bombardment of Front Line, N.36.D.7005. – N.36.D.5740.
on 6th September, 1916.

Unit.	Time	Task	Ammunition	Remarks
1½ Batteries, 6" How.	4 p.m.	N.36.D.7005 – N.36.D.5740	200	
D Battery, 173rd Brigade R.F.A.	"	N.36.D.7005 – 6615 and junction of Communication Trench and Support Trench at N.36.D.9813 & 9324.	200	One gun on each junction
D Battery, 172nd Brigade R.F.A.	"	N.36.D.6615 – 6.3 and junction of communication trench and support trench at N.36.D.8235.	200	do.
D Battery 86th Brigade R.F.A.	"	N.36.D.6.3 – 5740 and junction of communication trench and Support trench at N.36.D.7545 & 7350	200	do.
Left Centre Group 18pr Batteries	"	N.36.D.7005 – N.36.D.6325.	200 per Battery (150 A.X. 50 A)	Communication trenches to be sprayed with shrapnel.
Left Group 18pr Batteries	"	N.36.D.6325 – N.36.D.5740	–	do.
2" Trench Mortars.	"	Farm buildings	30.	

Note. After the salvos from all Batteries at 4 p.m. The rate of fire will be Trench Line 30 rounds, making the period of the Bombardment 50 minutes.

Appendix B.

Left Group Orders

1. A Bombardment of the enemy's front line, communication trenches and strong points on the 109 Brigade front will be carried out on the night of 15th/16th September 1916 in accordance with attached programme.

2. Rates of fire will be worked out by Battery Commanders to cover the whole period from 1.30 am till 12 noon 16.9.16

15th September 1916

sd/ H.C. Simpson.
Lieut Col
Commanding Left Group R.F.A.

Appendix B

A/173 Reserve line trench from 03/a52.80 to N30D 81.68

B/173 , Section on communication trench N36b 25.65 - N36b 85.78.
, " " " " N36b 85.79 - 02Sc 45.05
, " " " " 02Sc 45.05 - 02S2 15.20

C/173 , Section N30c 50.85 - N30d 33.10
, " N80b 33.10 - N30a 04.92
, " Strong point above N30a 85.60

D/173 , Section Strong point N36b 75.95
, " N30a 22.92

Appendix "F"   Copy No 8

Secret   Left Group Order No 3

O.C

1. A raid will take place on the night 30th Sept/1st October 1916

2. Zero time will be 10 p.m. and no gun is to fire before that hour except in case of emergency.

3. A box barrage will be formed by the left group as follows :-

   A/173 4 guns at T24a 1.9 Front line N36b 17.90 - N36a 91.18
          also Communication trench   N36a 91.18 - N36a 95.45

   A/173 2 guns Communication trench N36b 00.38 - N36b 38.48

   B/173 Support line N36b 00.38 - N36a 75.92.
        4 Guns to be on portion N36a 95.45 - N36a 79.69.

   C/173 Communication trench N36a 78.68 - N36a 58.65
         Front Line   N36a 58.65 - N36a 54.80.

   D/173 will block trench junctions as follows :-

       1 Gun   N36a 91.18
       1 "   N36b 00.38
       1 "   N36a 78.68
       1 "   N36a 58.65

4. Rate of fire. The normal rate of fire will be :-
   18 pdr batteries section fire 15 secs
   4.5 How   "   "   20 "

   but this can be altered at the discretion of battery commanders if the infantry call for a greater rate of fire.

5. The signal for the commencement of the bombardment will be 3 red rockets fired at N36a 49.20 and also the telephone.
       The bombardment will continue until the infantry signals by telephone to cease fire

6. Ammunition allowed.
   18 pdr batteries   700 rounds
   4.5" How Batteries   250 rounds

7. All batteries of the Group will be connected to A/173 at N32 b 5.0 who will pass on all orders from the front line.

8. Lieut G. A. Rickards will be in charge of all Artillery arrangements in the front trenches and will report to O.C. 10th R.I. Fusiliers at Cookers Farm at 3 p.m. on 30.9.16.

9. Watches will be synchronised at 9.0 p.m. with Brigade Headquarters.

10. Batteries will report opening and ceasing fire to Brigade Headquarters.

11. Acknowledge.

H. C. Pitt
Lieut Col
Commanding Left Group
36th Divisional Artillery

29th September 1916.

Copies to
1. 36th Div. Arty.
2. 109 Infy Brigade
3. A ⎫
4. B ⎬ 173
5. C ⎪
6. D ⎭
7. File
8.9. War Diary

War Diary.
of
173 Brigade R.F.A.
36 Division.
for
OCTOBER
1916

Army Form C. 2118.

37

WAR DIARY
or
INTELLIGENCE SUMMARY.
(Erase heading not required.)

Place: ARMENTIERES

Date	Hour	Summary of Events and Information	Remarks and references to Appendices
OCTOBER 1, 2 & 3		Operations Nil. Very quiet period.	
		Moves. On the nights of 1/2nd, 2nd/3rd fir batteries (B & C) of the Brigade moved out of their positions to relieve batteries of the 3rd Canadian Divl Arty in support of 16th Division.	
4	9 h	A/173 came into action by one section at A/153, the trench of the trench being thereof covered by A/173 (6 guns) at N 33 a 7.1, A 173 (2 guns) at T.18 c 4.6, and D/173, a 6.5 in. howr at N 27 a 3.1.	
5		Operations. A bombardment of enemy front line and support trenches (N 36 c 52.20 – 38.52 – 31.60 – 62.25) by French Mortars was carried out, with covering fire by 18pdrs & 4.5" Howrs on his own attacked.	appx A
		Hostile Artillery displayed considerable activity from 4.30 pm until 8.30 pm. A considerable number of rounds from 105 mm and 77 mm guns were fired along the whole of our front line & support & communication trench immediately in rear. Trench mortars were also active during this period, and some damage was done to trenches.	

Army Form C. 2118.

38

WAR DIARY
INTELLIGENCE SUMMARY.
(Erase heading not required.)

Instructions regarding War Diaries and Intelligence Summaries are contained in F. S. Regs, Part II. and the Staff Manual respectively. Title pages will be prepared in manuscript.

Place	Date	Hour	Summary of Events and Information	Remarks and references to Appendices
OCTOBER RANVOUTRE	6, 7, 8.		Operations Nil. Very quiet on both sides	
	9	1.30 am	Bombardment of enemy lines in N36a was carried out in support of a gas attack delivered along the whole of the Divisional Front. Hostile reply to Bombardment was very feeble.	Appx "B"
	10		Hostile Artillery. A few rounds from 77 and 105 mm guns were fired on our front line and area behind in N29 during the day. Our artillery retaliated.	
	11		A quiet day.	
	12		A raid was carried out by 9th R. Inns. Fus. Enemy trench mortars were very active during the raid	Appx "C"
	13		Operations Nil. A 105 mm gun was observed firing apparently from a spot about @ 21.c.3.5. This was reported to 40th H.A.G. otherwise Quiet.	
	14		Operations nil. The 105 mm gun mentioned on 13th inst was seen firing again. An 18 pdr battery fired a few rounds at @ 21.c.3.5 and the enemy gun ceased firing.	

39   Army Form C. 2118.

WAR DIARY
or
INTELLIGENCE SUMMARY.
(Erase heading not required.)

Place	Date	Hour	Summary of Events and Information	Remarks and references to Appendices
	OCTOBER.			
	14	Cont.	Considerable fair movement was observed.	
	15		Operations Nil. Trench mortars fairly active otherwise fairly Quiet	
	16		Operations nil. Both enemy Trench mortars and artillery fairly active	
	17		Operations. Our trench mortars carried out a bombardment App "D" of the enemy trenches assisted by the artillery lasting approximately one hour. — Enemy retaliation weak. Infantry report that our bombardment did considerable damage to Enemy's trenches.	
R A N C O U R T	18, 19		Operations nil. Very Quiet. Lt F Bowyer transferred to 111th HAG 2nd Army Rejoined the 19th	
	20, 21, 22		Again "amount of trench work appears to be in operation in enemy's lines — Hostile aeroplanes active — Quiet.	
	23		Enemy bombarded our line at V.12.a.0.0.2.8. with light trench mortars area at N.36.d.1.5. and N.36.a.5.1. with heavy mortars otherwise Quiet.	
	24		Operations nil. Hostile T.Ms active otherwise situation normal. Lt J. Yorke left for 2nd army Arty School at TiLAUGS an assistant instructor.	

Army Form C. 2118.

WAR DIARY
or
INTELLIGENCE SUMMARY.
(Erase heading not required.)

Instructions regarding War Diaries and Intelligence Summaries are contained in F. S. Regs., Part II. and the Staff Manual respectively. Title pages will be prepared in manuscript.

Place	Date	Hour	Summary of Events and Information	Remarks and references to Appendices
DRANOUTRE	October			
	25, 26, 27		Operations nil. Quiet but slight hostile T.M. activity	
	28		Operations nil. Quiet. A certain amount of movement behind enemy's lines	
	29		Operations. A raid was carried out by the 16th Division on our left. We cooperated with 3 18pdr batteries as stated. The enemy did not retaliate on our front. There was not successful. Third A.M. Harford PSK joined the brigade from England and was posted to D/173.	Appx "E"
	30		Operations nil. Quiet.	
	31		Operations. A raid was carried out by the 4th Royal Irish Rifles & covered by N. hoz. temp as shown in Appendix F. Owing to one of the armoured strafes not exploring the raiding party was unable to penetrate the wire at one of the intended points of entry.	Appx "F"

H.R. [signature]
Lieut Col Cdg
OC. 173 B.A.C.

SECRET.   App^x B   Copy No 5

Amendment to
Left Group Operation Order No 6

1. Owing to an alteration in the
point of entry into enemy lines
the Right Box Barrage will be:—

Hows guns. 1 gun N36a 92.30 – 85.60
Battery   1 gun N36a 62.50 – 85.60
           1 gun N36a 92.32 – 87.20

The Left Box Barrage will be
Battery.   1 gun N36a 55.80 – 75.75
           1 gun N30c 50.15 – 70.20
How guns   1 gun N36a 75.75 – N30c 70.20

D/173 will shoot as follows:—
Left Barrage. 1 gun on N36a 75.75
               1 gun on N30c 70.20

Right Barrage 1 gun on N36b 00.35
               1 gun on N36a 85.60

Acknowledge by wire

        Edwards
        Major R.F.A.
8/10/16 Com^{dg} Left Group

Secret

Appendix "B"

[Lens Attack?]
Supplementary Orders
Operation Order No 6

1. Zero hour will be 1.30 am [date] 8/9 October 1916.

2. Right Battalion will leave N36a 45.25 and [enemy?] [?] line at N36a 55.35.
   [?] Battalion will leave N30c 40.04 and [enter enemy?] line at N30c 55.10

   Time - X + 1 hour 15 minutes

3. Barrage
   Right Barrage as previously ordered.
   The Barrage for the [?] Battalion, is called for will be

   1 gun Battery   N36a 50.90 - 70.92
   1 gun   N30c 50.30 - 60.30
   1 gun [Aunt?]   N30c 60.30 - N36a 70.92
   D173 1 gun N36a 72.95   1 gun N30c 58.40

4. Ammunition allotment for bombardment

   200 rounds per 18 pr Battery
   200   "   " 4.5" How

   Barrages, if called for, will be additional to the above.

5. Rates of fire:-
   Bombardment Bd's will maintain a steady rate of fire to cover the whole period.
   Barrage as called for [?] the fire [?] [?]

6. All other orders remain as in Operation Order No 6

7. O.C. A/173 will arrange direct with
Batalion Commanders and ascertain details
re Canaux

Acknowledge.

Issued at 11.30 P.M.
8.10.16

Major R.F.A.
Commanding 7th Group

Copies to
1. 31st Div Arty
2. 109th Bde
3. C/173
4. D/173
5. D.T.M.O.
6.7 War Diary
8. File

Secret (Page 2)
Appendix B   Copy No 8

Left Group Order No 5

1. The gas cylinders installed in all 3 Bde Sectors will be discharged tonight if the weather conditions are favourable.

    Zero hour is 1 a.m.

    If at any time prior to that hour conditions are considered definitely unfavourable, the following telegram will be sent from D.H.Q:-

    "The answer is No"

    This will cancel the attack.

2. The enemy's front and support lines on the front of the Gas Attack will be bombarded by medium and light Trench Mortars and Rifle Grenades. Machine Guns will continue from plus 4 minutes to plus 25 minutes.

3. Each Battalion in the line will send out patrols at plus 1 hour 15 minutes and will endeavour to investigate the effects of the gas.

4. Box barrages will be put up by the Group Artillery if required by raiding patrols.

5. Watches will be synchronised with Group H.Q. at 12 midnight.

6. No information or instructions regarding these operations will be sent by telephone except in code.

7. From 8 p.m all wires will be reserved for tactical purposes.

8. Bombardment x 4' to x 25'

    D 172 will block the following points

    N 36 a 80.72

    N 36 a 88.60

　　　　　N36b 00.80
　　　　　N36a 95.45
　　　　　N36b 20.92
　　　　　N36b 25.35

If a box barrage is called for by the Right Battalion D/73 will put 2 guns on the following
　　　　　N36a 95.42
　　　　　N36a 88.50

If Left Battalion call for barrage D/173 will put 2 guns on the following
　　　　　N36a 80.76
　　　　　36a 75.90

Bombardment X4′ to X25′

A/173 will fire on

　　C.I. (1) N36a 80.90 – 85.90
　　　　　　N36a 85.75 – 90.70
　　　　　　N36a 85.30 – N36b 15.35　} Battery
　　　　　　N36a 90.10 – N36b 25.30
　　　　　　N36a 80.70 – N36b 20.00　} Hants
　　　　　　N36b 10.70 – N36b 50.15　　 Section

Box Barrage
Right Battalion
　　Hants Guns　1 gun　N36a 92.30 – 80.45
　　Battery　　　1 gun　N36a 62.80 – 80.45
　　　　　　　　1 gun　N36a 92.32 – 89.20

Left Battalion
　　Battery　　　1 gun　N36a 54.65 – 90.70
　　　　　　　　1 gun　N36a 72.92 – 85.95
　　Hants guns　 1 gun　N36a 80.72 – 72.92

　　　　　　　　　　　　} 3rd Section of
　　　　　　　　　　　　 Battery will be
　　　　　　　　　　　　 used for whichever
　　　　　　　　　　　　 Barrage is
　　　　　　　　　　　　 most urgent.

9　Ammunition allowance
　　　18 pdr Battery – 150 rounds
　　　4.5″ How Battery　200　"

Appendix B (Page 3)

Battery Commanders will arrange to cover the period of bombardment at gunfire 30 secs for 2 hours. Dutch guns will fire "Gunfire" 30 secs the balance of the allotment being kept in case a barrage is called for.

10. Calls for barrages will be sent through A/173
   Left barrage telephone "Please barrage"
   Right   "   "   "Please barrage"
   also two Red rockets from N36a4o.35

11. In the event of barrages being called for "Cease Fire" will be sent by the Infantry to A/173 who will transmit to D/173 and report to Group H.Q.

12. Medium Trench Mortars will bombard the enemy support line over the front covered by the gas discharge. Rate of fire as fast as possible.

Issued at 9 pm.   Major R.H.G.
5.10.16   Commanding Left Group

Copies to
1. 38th D.A.
2.3.4. 109th Infy Bde
5. D.T.M.O.
6. A/173
7. D/173
8.9 War Diary

Secret

Appendix C

Copy No.

Left Front 38th Div Arty

Operation Order No 9

1. The 9th R. Innis Fusiliers will Raid the enemy trenches on the night of the 11/12th

2. Zero time will be notified later and no gun will be fired before that time

3. B.C's will arrange to have an Officer in their B.P's or other suitable places for observing One Red Asteroid Rocket which will be fired from N29a 9500 this and or telephone will be the signal for formation of a Box Barrage

    Telephone 'This' B/173

    Order to cease fire will be telephoned by the Infantry

4. Ammunition allowance
    - 275 rounds per Battery 18 pdr
    - 200 " " " 4.5 Hows

5. Rate of fire G.F. 30" 18 pdrs.
    " 40" 4.5 Hows

6. Batteries will fire on following trenches forming a Box Barrage

    A/173   2 guns
        N30c 5215 - 6818 - 9208
        2 guns (shrine)
    N30c 9208 - 9030
    N30c 7815 - 7066 (to prevent movement in open)
    B/173 N30c 7066 - 9030
    C/173 N30c 1262 - 5872 - 7066
    D/173 Will block the following junctions
        N30c 5872 7066 6818 9030

7. B.C's will report to this office opening and cessation of fire

8. Watches will be synchronised at time to be notified later

(sd) G. Edwards
Major R.F.A
Commanding Left Group
R.F.A

Copies to
1. 38 Div Arty   4. A/173   7. D/173
2. 109 Infy Bde   5. B/173   8. War Diary
3. 9th R.I.F.   6. C/173   9. File

APPENDIX "D"

Secret   Copy No.

3rd Brigade Order No. 10

1. A Trench Mortar Bombardment in which all Mortars in the Brigade will take part will be carried out on Tuesday 17th October 1916.

2. Schedule will be as under:

   Time of Fire

   Heavy Mortars   Artillery

   ao
   0 to + 15   Bombardment   + 2 to + 15
   +15 to +25   Interval   + 15 to + 25
   " 25 " " 40 Bombardment   " 25 to " 40
   " 40 " " 45 Interval   " 40 to + 45
   " 45 " " 65 Bombardment   " 45 to + 65

3. O.C. Divl. Signals will send runners from O.P. to a.m. to Brigade and no wires will be sown under by the infantry until 3 p.m.

4. Targets:

   V.36   1st period   Bombardment   N.26.a. 1050
          2nd   N.26.a. 0552
          3rd   N.26.a. 0513

   X.36   5" & 9" Battery

   1 gun   Bombardment   N.26.a. 0045 N.26.a. 0063
                         N.26.a. 0063 N.26.a. 0550

   1 gun   N.26.a. 0045 0063
                         N.26.a. 9516 9545

   1 gun   N.26.a. 9545 9516
                         N.26.a. 9862 8862

   1 gun   N.26.a. 9242 8852
                         N.26.a. 9240 8510

5. The Left Group will give covering fire as follows:

   A/173 Battery include N.26.a. 7030 N.36.a. 4070
   A/173 "   N.36.a. 0082 N.26.a. 9230
   B/173 3 guns   C.   N.26.a. 7898 N.36.a. 2860

Secret   # Appendix "E"   Copy No

Left Group Order No 12

28.10.16

1. A raid will be carried out by 16th Division at a time to be notified later.

2. The following points are to be raided
     N30 a 2.70 & N20c 8.5

3. The following Artillery action will be taken by 36th Divisional Artillery in support of the raid.

4. B/173 will support the raid as follows
     Zero to plus 2 minutes   Barrage front line
                                                N30a 45.87 - N30a 80.32

     Plus 2 minutes to cease fire   Cup Lake B.T.
                                                    N30a 47.38 - N30a 95.40

5. A/173 and C/173 will take action as in table below

Time	Unit	Task
Zero to plus 2 minutes	A/173	Barrage front line N30c 35.53 - N30c 17.60
Zero to plus 2 minutes	C/173	Barrage front line N30c 17.60 - N30c 10.80
Plus 2 mins to plus 18 mins	A/173	Barrage to creep at 50 yds per minute to line N30c 35.58 - N30c 50.60 - N30c 45.70 where it remains
Plus 2 mins to plus 18 mins	C/173	Barrage to creep at 50 yds per minute to line N30c 45.70 - N30c 35.80 - N30c 10.80 where it remains

6. Rate of fire

     B/173   Zero to plus 2 minutes   Gun fire 10 seconds
                Plus 2 mins to plus 20 mins   "   30   "
                Plus 20 "   "   30 "   "   1 minute
                Plus 30 " onwards   "   2 "

     A/173 and C/173
          Zero to plus 2 minutes   Gun fire 10 seconds

plus 2 minutes to plus 15 minutes Gun fire 30 seconds

7. B/173 will be notified by Group H.Q when to cease firing
8. Watches will be synchronised at a time to be notified later from Group H.Q.
9. No reference to these operations is to be made over the telephone.
10. Telephone communication will be maintained between Left Group 36th Div Arty and Right Group 16th Div Arty
11. Acknowledge

28.10.16

Lt Col R.F.A.
Commanding Left Group

Copies to
1. A/173
2. C/173
3. B/173
4. D/173
5. 36th Div Arty
6. 16th Div Arty
7. Right Group 16th Div Arty
8. 109 Infy Bde
9. File

Secret

Appendix "F"

Copy No

Left Group Order No 11

28.10.16

1. A raid will be carried out by 14th Royal Irish Rifles on the night 31st Oct/1st Nov at a time to be notified later.

2. Points of entry
   N36a 56.63 and N36a 56.90

3. Fire will not be opened unless called upon. If Artillery support is required it will be given in the form of a box barrage as below and the signal that it is required will be a succession of Green Verey Lights fired from N36a 55.60 repeated by a green rocket from our own front line.

4. The Infantry carrying out the raid will establish blocking parties as follows:-
   N36a 60.58
   " 65.60
   " 70.60
   " 70.62
   " 68.74
   " 58.83
   " 53.87

5. The raiding party will remain in the German Trenches for half an hour.

6. The box barrage will be as follows:-

   (4 guns) C/173 Enfilade N30c 55.02 – N30c 73.02 N36a 95.97
   C/173 Barrage N36a 95.97 – N36a 95.85 – N36b 13.72
   D/173 (Howitzers) Enfilade N36b 13.72 – N36b 22.58
   C/173 Enfilade N36b 22.58 – N36a 67.28
   D/173 will block the following points
   N30c 69.19   N36b 25.80
   N36b 25.88   N36b 00.40

   X 36 Medium T.M. Battery will fire as follows
   1 gun about N36a 88.20
   1 "   "   N30c 48.30

6" Hows will cooperate as follows
   N36b 25.80   N36b 75.95

7. At zero minus 5 minutes the Medium T.M's will fire a few rounds in the enemy second line trench between
   N36a 90.48 – N30a 72.05
   C/173 will cooperate to cover flashes

8. Rate of fire
   18 pdrs 1 am fire 30 seconds
   4.5" How.   40   "

9. Watches will be synchronised with Group H.Q. at a time to be notified later.

10. Machine gun at N36a 58.38 will be dealt with previously by 6" Hows

11. No conversation concerning these operations is to take place over the telephone.

12. N36 7 (Southern half) N31 8 N36 11 (Northern half) N30 1, N30 2 (Southern half) will be shelled

13. Acknowledge

14. Zero Time 3.50 am 31st Oct / 1st Nov.

28.10.16   Lt Col R.F.A.
Copies to   O.C. Left Group
  1. A/173   R.F.A.
  2. B/173
  3. C/173
  4. D/173
  5. X36 T.M.B.
  6. 38th Div Arty
  7. 109 Infy Bde
  8. File

Appendix 'A'   Copy No 6

Secret

Left Group Order No 5

1. There will be a bombardment of the enemy front line system, by the Left Group on Thursday 8th inst beginning at 8.30 a.m.

2. The following time table will be observed

    8.30 - 8.40 Bombardment
    8.40 - 8.45 Interval
    8.45 - 8.55 Bombardment
    8.55 - 9.25 Silent interval
    9.25 - 9.35 Bombardment

3. Watches will be synchronised at 7.30 a.m. O.C. X/36 and V/36 T.M. Batteries will receive correct time from the Artillery Liaison Officer with the Right Battalion at 8.0 a.m.

   The Liaison Officer will synchronise his watch at Battalion Headquarters at 7.30 a.m.

4. The targets will be as follows

   1 gun V/36 Heavy Trench Mortar Battery.
   2nd line N36a 92.78 to N36a 92.80

   X/36 Medium Trench Mortar Battery with other Mortars 109th Infy Bde -

   Parallelogram N30c 82.20 - 38.83
                     - 50.40 - 62.25

   A/173 Communication Trenches -
           N30c 30.25 - 62.48
                40.82 - 61.30
                35.80 - 81.58

and 2nd line to 20.X.15.16

D/173 から line from N.30.c.5.2.20 to N.30.c.28.35.

The detached section of B/173 will fire from
8.30 to 8.55 and from 9.25 to 9.35
on support line from N.30.c.12.28 to 50.60.

5. Ammunition allowed.

Trench Mortar Batteries, as much as
possible in the time.

    A/173 (6 guns)   150 rounds
    (detached section)   60
    D/173   150

6. Rates of fire will be worked out by Battery
commanders so as to cover the whole period of
the bombardment.

7.   Trenches N.31. 8. 9. 10 and 11
               N.30. 1 and 2 and
               N.29. 1
        will be cleared.

Acknowledge.

                                   G. Edwards
Sent at
11.10.16   Major R.F.A.
to pencils   Commanding Left Group
  1. 34th Div Arty
  2. 102 Inf Bde
  3. D.T.M.O.
  4. A/173
  5. D/173
  6. 7 Hardings
  8. File

No 13 36

WAR DIARY.

for

173rd BRIGADE, R.F.A.

MONTH ending NOV. 30, 1916

Army Form C. 2118.

173 Bde RFA.
36 Div.

WAR DIARY
or
INTELLIGENCE SUMMARY.
(Erase heading not required.)

Instructions regarding War Diaries and Intelligence Summaries are contained in F.S. Regs., Part II. and the Staff Manual respectively. Title pages will be prepared in manuscript.

Place	Date	Hour	Summary of Events and Information	Remarks and references to Appendices
DRANOUTRE	NOVEMBER		Operations nil	
	1,2		uneventful -	
	3		The morning was very quiet. There was slight T.M. activity by the Boches on our right. The enemy later he retaliated and some boots on to our Group front. Two T.M.s were located & dealt with successfully by our Howitzers & T.M.s. A big explosion was reported at N36.c.9520 (sent in to the Enemy lines as the result of our fire	
	4		The day on the whole was very misty and stannistican much impeded	
		3.15pm	A demonstration by our T.M.s. took place. three fire being covered by our 18 pdrs. Our Howitzers dealing with hostile T.M.s firing in retaliation to our fire	See Appendix A
			During the early part of the afternoon from about 3.05 p.m. onward the Battery and a few 18 m.m on the road running along N33a + also at N33c. No damage to men or material was sustained	
	5	5pm	The Remainder of the day was quiet, enemy continuing throughout the night. On the whole quite E & D Batteries dealt with hostile fature observed at O.25.d.50.25.	

T.134. Wt. W703-776. 500000. 4/15. Sir J. C. & S.

173 Bde RFA
36 Div.

Army Form C. 2118.

WAR DIARY
or
INTELLIGENCE SUMMARY.
(Erase heading not required.)

Place	Date	Hour	Summary of Events and Information	Remarks and references to Appendices
DRANOUTRE	NOVEMBER			
	6		The weather during the morning was very dull but the afternoon was clear. Observation very good.	
		6.50am	'D' Bty fired on working party observed at O.25.d. 50.25. In each case	
		10.30am	the party was dispersed.	
		10.a.m	'B' Bty reported T.M. "Scream". Hostile artillery was rather active during the morning. A flash was observed reported on by 'D' Bty. Trench trenches taken by 'B' Bty. These went and on to H.A.Q. In connection with this firing the enemy was seen signalling by means of Very lights & Rockets.	
	7		The afternoon & evening were quiet. The day was rather wet & little in the way of operations could be carried out. During the afternoon our guns effectively silenced hostile T.M.s	
	8		A very quiet day. During the day there was no have been obliged to suspend offensive operations for a few days.	
		9.10 9.iii 12	Very quiet, opened ruma nil. The order regarding the suspension of operations received & the batteries carry on	

173 Brigade R.F.A.
36 Div.

WAR DIARY
or
INTELLIGENCE SUMMARY.
(Erase heading not required.)

Army Form C. 2118.

Place	Date	Hour	Summary of Events and Information	Remarks and references to Appendices
GRANDCOURT	NOVEMBER			
	12 13th		A normal state of war. Quiet uneventful. Enemy artillery was active during the afternoon and sent Shrapnel over the roads about our Battery Positions. The damage was caused to the personnel or materiel. A hostile T.M. fired 3 rounds and our sector but was promptly silenced by our own Machine T.M's	
	15	11.30 a.m.	A Trench Mortar demonstration was carried out according to previously arranged order [Appendix B]. It proved successful & some good work was apparent. The enemy retaliation was very slight. The hostile T.M's which attempted to fire were promptly dealt with by the batteries. The batteries carried out counter fire during the operations	Appendix B
	16	10 p.m.	Operations: A raid was carried out by 109 Inf Brigade supported by an artillery fire-barrage. The raid was entirely successful, the prisoners being taken. Several germans killed and enemy trenches damaged - Our casualties were	Appendix C

WAR DIARY
or
INTELLIGENCE SUMMARY.

(Erase heading not required.)

17   Bde   R.F.A.   Army Form C. 2118.
36 Div.

Place	Date	Hour	Summary of Events and Information	Remarks and references to Appendices
DRANOUTRE	November			
	16 Contd		Styli & the enemy observation turret –	
	17, 18		Operations nil. Quiet day, weather misty, observation difficult. Enemy Trench mortars were active between 1.30 to 2 pm, about 8 mortars being in action opposite this Brigade front.	
	19		Quiet, fog prevents observation of enemy's lines.	
	20, 21, 22		Operations. A combined bombardment of enemy lines was carried out as shown in appendix "D". Considerable damage was done to enemy's lines. Enemy trench mortars replied vigorously during the bombardment but this artillery showed little activity till after the bombardment ceased when he opened fire for about 10 minutes with probably 4 batteries.	
	23			
	24		Enemy's artillery was more active than usual. Hostile trench mortars were abnormally active between 1.30 pm and 3.30 pm. They were effectively prevented by our artillery. The 154th Batteries of the group concentrating on each T.M. as it became active	

DRAFT

Army Form C. 2118.

173 Bde R.F.A.
36 Div.

WAR DIARY
or
INTELLIGENCE SUMMARY.
(Erase heading not required.)

Place: DRANOUTRE

Date	Hour	Summary of Events and Information	Remarks and references to Appendices
NOVEMBER			
24 contd		Find 2 rounds gunfire, and the H.S. O.P. now batteries fire up to 30 rounds on each emplacement. Every known T.M. on the Brigade front has been given a name beginning with 'S' (such as SUSAN, SATAN, SPITFIRE &c) and whenever any of them become active the "So and So active" is immediately telephoned to all batteries by whichever battery receives the report first, and all guns are concentrated on it. — Hostile Artillery between (77mm, 105mm and 150mm) was fired mostly on front and support lines. Hostile T.M.s was active during the same period. They were effectively dealt with by our artillery by the same means as on the 23rd & 24th inst.	
25		Uneventful except that an enemy aeroplane apparently hit by our AA guns stemmed past our (?) hutting position. Spells group only a few feet from the ground apparently missing your endeavour to rise. I did no (?) however and	
26.			

WAR DIARY
or
INTELLIGENCE SUMMARY.
(Erase heading not required.)

173 Bde R.F.A.
36 Div.

Army Form C. 2118.

Place	Date	Hour	Summary of Events and Information	Remarks and references to Appendices
DRANOUTRE	NOVEMBER			
	26. Cont.		and succeeded in making off in the direction of the german lines. Owing to their men in the plane Operations nil. Quiet. Thick mist observation impossible.	
	27.28.29		Quiet. Thick mist observation impossible.	
	30		Operations. A combined trench mortar bombardment was carried out by this division in conjunction with a bombardment by the Celtic group and assisted by one 4.5 How battery and one 18 pdr section of this group. The bombardment was carried out in four periods of 15 minutes each, with 5 minutes interval between each. Bombardment began at 2 p.m. Enemy's retaliation was feeble, only one T.M. being reported active on this brigade front. Altogether 20 rounds from hostile field guns were fired on this front during the bombardment. A westerly wind prevailed during the bombardment so the effect of our fire could not be ascertained.	

Original signed/REH
Commdg 173 Bde RFA
30.11.16

Secret   **Appendix "A"**   Copy No

Left Group Order No

1. A bombardment of the enemy's lines will take place on the 4th inst.

2. Zero time will be 3.15 p.m. and the duration of the bombardment will be 15 minutes.

3. The T.M's of the Left Group will act as follows

4. V/36 Heavy T.M. Battery

   1 Gun will fire on STINKER (N36a 70.70) Hostile Trench Mortar emplacement

5. X/36 Medium T.M battery will fire on

   Enemy Trench Tramway System between N36a 18.50 and N36a 65.75.

6. The Heavy T.M's will fire as fast as possible consistent with good laying.

   The Medium T.M's will maintain a rate of fire of one round per gun per minute.

7. The following trenches will be cleared
   N36 8, 9, 10

   The O.B. V/36 will personally satisfy himself that there are no infantry in his line of fire or in the danger zone on either side. He will report all clear to Group H.Q. before opening fire

8. Acknowledge

Secret

Appendix B   Copy No 10

Left Group Order No 15

1. A Trench Mortar bombardment will take place on 15th inst

2. Zero time will be 11.30 a.m

3. Times of firing will be as follows:-

　　Medium T.M. Battery

　　　11 30 – 11 45　Bombardment
　　　11 45 – 11 50　Pause
　　　11 50 – 12 05　Bombardment
　　　12 05 – 12 10　Pause
　　　12 10 – 12 25　Bombardment

Heavy T.M and Artillery of Group will keep up a steady rate of fire from 11 30 a.m to 12 30 p.m

4. Medium T.M battery will fire as follows:-

　　1 gun on N30c 38.47　MG
　　1　　　N36a 48.97　MG in Gap
　　1　　　N36a 60.40　MG in NOSE

Heavy T.M will fire
　　N36a 90.50

D/193 will commence bombardment as follows:-

　　One gun on SPITFIRE
　　　　　　　STOKER
　　　　　　　STRAFFER
　　　　　　　SATAN

and will be ready to switch a section at once on to any enemy T.M which becomes active

18 pdr batteries will bombard any Trench Mortar emplacements in their own zones

5. Rates of Fire

　　Medium T.M.　2 rounds per gun per minute
　　Heavy　T.M.　as fast as possible consistent with good laying

     4·5" Hows   Gun fire 40 secs
     18 pdr   A steady rate for 1 hour

6. Ammunition allowed
   Medium T.M and Heavy T.M   As much as possible
               to be fired
     4·5" Hows   150 rounds BX
     18 pdr   75   —   AX

7. The G.O.C 109th Infantry Brigade has been asked to allow the 109th Light T.M. Battery to cooperate.

8. A report of the bombardment is to reach Group H.Q by evening orderly

9. The G.O.C 109th Infantry Brigade has been asked to clear the following trenches
   N 36 7
   N 36 8
   N 36 9
   N 36 11

10. Acknowledge

Issued at 12 noon
14.11.16

             A Lloyd 2/Lt
             for Lt Col R.A.
             Commdg Left Group
               R.F.A

Copies to
1. 36 Div Arty
2. 109th Infy Bde
3. A/173
4. B/173
5. C/173
6. D/173
7. X 36 T.M
8. V 36 T.M
9. File
10, 11 War Diary

Secret

Appendix C

Copy No 10
Reference 1/10000 map
WYTSCHAETE
Edition 3E

Left Group Order No 144

1. A raid will be carried out by 109th Infy Brigade

2. Zero time will be 7.45 pm 14th November 1916

3. The points of entry will be as follows:-

   No 1 Party N30c 50 05
   No 2 Party N30c 50 18
   No 3 Party N30c 45 27
   No 4 Party N30c 41 44

4. Blocking points will be as follows:-

   (i)   N36a 49 93 (just north of SAP)
   (ii) N36a 53 93 (Tramway)
   (iii) N36a 58 97 (Trench Junction)
   (iv) N30c 69 08 (Trench Junction)
   (v)   N30c 62 20 (Trench Junction)
   (vi) N30c 51 49 (Trench)
   (vii) N30c 33 55 (Mine shafts)

5. There will be no preliminary bombardment but an Artillery box barrage as under will be called for by special signal when required. The probable duration of fire will be 15 hours.

   Up to and including date of raid Medium TMs will cut wire and bombard enemy's front line covering fronts of raid.

6. The arrangements for the box barrage are as follows:-

   A/173 (4 guns) On whole communication trench N36a 55 18 - N36b 20 88

   A/153 (4 guns) Barrage N36b 20 88 - N36b 11 98 - N30d 13 02 (beginning of hedge) - N30d 04 15 (along hedge)

   C/173 (6 guns) Barrage N30d 04 15 - N30c 91 31 (Junction hedge and trench) - N30d 00 55 (Junction of Path and trench)

   1 Section 16th Div Arty Barrage from N30d 00 55 - N30c 96 58 (Trench Junction)

1 Section 18th Div Batty on palisade path N30d 00 55 - N30c 87 75

E/173 (6 guns)   on palisade from N30c 96 77 - N30c 87 75
                  N30c 29 89 (trench junction) - N30c 07 87

A/173 (detached section) 1 gun on N30d 00 55 (junction of path and trench)
                         1 "   N30c 91 78 (trench junction)

D/173 Will bombard following points:
        1 gun N36a 55 19
        1 " N30c 91 31 (junction of lady's strand)
        1 " N30c 91 78 (trench junction)
        1 " N30c 07 87

6 Hows will fire on the following points:
        1 gun on Bone Roads N31b 23 95
        1 "   BONE POINT N31b 72 95
        1 "   RAG POINT N30d 22 93
        1 "   trench junction N30c 18 03

X 36 Medium Trench Mortars will fire as follows:
        1 gun on N36a 55 40
        1 "   N36a 59 49

7 Rates of fire
        18 pdr Gun fire 20 secs
        4.5 Hows   30 "
        6 Hows 1 round per gun per 2 minutes
        2 T.M's 1 round per gun per minute

8 The signal for the Artillery barrage will be a telephone message direct from the front dump to Group HQ

Group HQ will inform all batteries

A green rocket will also be fired from the front of the BULL RING N30c 35 18

An officer will be detailed by D/173 to observe for this signal from LONE HOUSE this officer to be in direct telephonic communication with Group HQ.

9. The order to cease fire will be sent from Group H.Q.

10. No conversation regarding these operations will be carried on over the telephone.

11. Watches will be synchronised from Group HQ at 9 a.m. 3 p.m. and 6 p.m on 14th inst.

12. The O.C. 109th Infantry Brigade has been asked to clear the following trenches
    N 36 8
    N 36 9
    Southern half of N 36 10

13. Acknowledge.

Issued at 6 p.m.
10.11.16

H. Kennedy /t
for
Lt Col R.F.A.
Commanding Left Group
R.F.A.

Copy No 1. 36th Div Arty
    2. 109th Infty Bde
    3. A/173
    4. B/173
    5. C/173
    6. D/173
    7. X 36 T.M.B.
    8. O.C. Centre Group 36th Div Arty
    9. O.C. Right Group 16th
    10. War Diary
    11. File

LATER. (1) The above raid is postponed till 16th Inst.

(2) Zero time will be 10 p.m.

H. Kennedy /t
for H.O?

Secret

Appendix "D"

Copy No 13

Amendment No 1 to Left Group Order No 16

1. Para No 2 is to be amended. Only one Heavy T.M. will engage N36b 2.3.

2. One Mortar V/36 will engage MORTAR FARM N36d 70.25

3. The G.O.C. 107th Infantry Brigade has been asked to clear the following trenches
    N36 1
    N36 2
    N36 3 (Southern half)
    T66 (Northern half)

    The O.C. V/36 T.M.B. will detail an Officer to see that nobody except those specially detailed is in the danger zone and will report all clear to Group H.Q. before opening fire.

4. Para 8 will be amended as follows:-
    For N36 5.6.7.8.9.10 read
    N36 6 (~~Southern half~~)
    N36 7
    N36 8
    N36 9
    N36 10

5. Acknowledge

H.C.P.
Lt Col R.F.A.
Commanding Left Group
R.F.A.

Issued at 9 a.m.
22.11.16

Copies to
1. H.Q 36th Div Arty
2. 109 Bde
3. 9/73
4. 8/73
5. 6/73
6. D/73
7. Centre Group 36 Div Arty
8. X/36 T.M.B.
9. V/36 T.M.B.
10. Right Group 36 Div Arty
11. 107 Bde
12. 108 Bde
13. War Diary
14.
15. File

Secret   Copy No 14

Left Group Order No 16

1. There will be a combined bombardment of enemy's trenches on Thursday 23rd inst beginning at 11.30 a.m. when the following points will be engaged
   (a) Concrete dugouts along tramway at N36a 60.47
   (b) " " " " " " N36a 56.62
   (c) " " " " " " N36a 53.80
   (d) Dugouts at N36b 2.3

2. The following will be the distribution for engaging the above objectives:-
   (a) Objective 3 Stokes Mortars of 108th Brigade
                  2 Medium   "   X/36 Battery
   (b)   3 Stokes   "   107 Brigade
                  2 Medium   "   Z/36 Battery
   (c)   3 Stokes   "   109 Brigade
                  2 Medium   "   Y/36 Battery
   (d)   2 Heavy   "   V/36 Battery

3. The time table for the bombardment will be as follows:-
   11.30 – 11.48 Bombardment
   11.48 – 12.05 Interval
   12.05 – 12.20 Bombardment
   12.20 – 12.40 Interval
   12.40 – 12.55 Bombardment

4. The batteries of the Left Group plus A/153 will cooperate as follows:-

   A/153 will engage SUSAN, SALLY, SARAH, TOM
   A/173   "   "   STINKER, SATAN, SIDNEY, SAVOY
   C/173   "   "   STOKER, SIBERIA, STRAFFER
                      SAUSAGE, SAXON, STEPHEN.
   B/173   "   "   SOPHIE, SARDINE, SPITFIRE
                      SPREE, SYKES.
   D/173 2 guns   SYBIL
   D/173   "   SAXON - This section will be in
                      readiness to turn onto any hostile
                      T.M. which may open fire

5. Ammunition allowed - this allotment is not to be exceeded

   A/173   90 rounds
   A/153   90 rounds
   B/173   120 "
   C/173   100 "
   D/173   100 "

   18 pdr batteries will fire 75% A.X.

6. Batteries will open fire 2 minutes before each period of bombardment is timed to commence and will maintain a steady rate of fire during the period.

7. Watches will be synchronised at 9 a.m. from Group H.Q.

8. The G.O.C. 109th Infy Bde has been asked to clear the following trenches:
   N 36 5 - 6 - 7 - 8 - 9 - 10
   O.C. V/36 T.M. Battery will see that nobody except those specially detailed is in the danger zone and will report all clear to Group H.Q. before opening fire.

9. Acknowledge

21.11.16

Lt Col R.F.A.
Commdg Left Group R.F.A.

Copies to
1. H.Q. 36th Div Arty
2. H.Q. 109th Bde
3. A/173
4. B/173
5. C/173
6. D/173
7. Centre Group 36 Div Arty
8. X 36 T.M.B.
9. V/36 T.M.B.
10. Right Group 36 Div Arty
11. 107th Bde
12. 108th Bde
13. War Diary
14. "
15. File

WAR DIARY
173rd BRIGADE. R.F.A.
36th DIVISION.

December 1st. 1916 to
31st. 1916.

Army Form C. 2118.

173 Brigade R.F.A.
36 Div.

WAR DIARY
or
INTELLIGENCE SUMMARY.
(Erase heading not required.)

Instructions regarding War Diaries and Intelligence
Summaries are contained in F. S. Regs., Part I.
and the Staff Manual respectively. Title pages
will be prepared in manuscript.

Place	Date	Hour	Summary of Events and Information	Remarks and references to Appendices
December				
	1st, 2nd, 3rd, 4th, 5th		Operations nil — Quiet — Thick mist obscured enemy's lines — Operations nil — Hostile artillery and TMs displayed rather more activity than usual. Our 15 pdr + 4.5 Hows dealt effectively with TMs.	
	5th		The 47th Infy. Bde took over the front occupied by the 109 Bde — This is the front normally covered by us, which is continue to cover for the time being, coming under the orders of the VIIIth 16th Divisional artillery for tactical purposes and becoming their Right Group (The 36 Div artily. artillery Group covering the SPANBROEK Sector (namely ourselves) is renamed the SPANBROEK Group. In order to avoid confusion the Group covering the SPANBROEK Left Group.	
	6,7		Operations nil. Quiet with the exception of a short bombardment each afternoon by enemy TMs which were in each case effectively punished by 18 pdrs and 4.5"hows of this brigade.	
	8,9,10		Operations nil. The enemy is beginning to show a little more artillery activity on this front.	
	11,12,13		The enemy have slackened the practice of carrying out a short	

DRANOUTRE

Army Form C. 2118.

173 Bde R.F.A
36 Div.

WAR DIARY
or
INTELLIGENCE SUMMARY.
(Erase heading not required.)

Instructions regarding War Diaries and Intelligence Summaries are contained in F.S. Regs., Part II. and the Staff Manual respectively. Title pages will be prepared in manuscript.

Place	Date	Hour	Summary of Events and Information	Remarks and references to Appendices
DRANOUTRE	DECEMBER			
	13 contd		Trench mortar bombardment before sunset and 4 pm almost daily	
	14,15		Operations nil. Quiet –	
	16		Operations nil. Hostile artillery and TM's much more active than usual. Hostile enemy artillery was active & green lights were put up from the German line – This is thought to have been an indication to his artillery to lengthen their range as some rounds were observed to fall short. Enemy registered 24 AM Howitzer	
	17.18		Enemy artillery and TM's were again active between 2.30 and 3 pm	
	19		Quiet – 2/o R.F. Sharp and 2/Lt R.E. Jones joined the Brigade	
	20		Quiet. The enemy appears to be registering by aeroplane. Several planes were up –	
	21		Operations nil. Hostile TM's very active at 3.45 for 20 minutes	
	22.23		Quiet	
	24		Operations nil. Skylib hostile artillery and trench mortar activity – It being a clear day hostile aeroplanes were active	

WAR DIARY or INTELLIGENCE SUMMARY.

173 Bde RFA
36 Div

Army Form C. 2118.

Place: DRANOUTRE

Date	Hour	Summary of Events and Information	Remarks and references to Appendices

DECEMBER

25, 26, 27. Quiet
A bombardment of enemy trenches by trench mortars carried out by artillery was carried out as set shown in Appendix A by artillery retaliation to our bombardments was near as the Enemy T.Ms bombarded our trenches heavily during the first half of our bombardment though during the latter half they were comparatively quiet.
The relief of this brigade by the 180 Bde R.F.A began on sections of each battery being relieved by the incoming brigade.

App "A"

28. The relief by the 180 Bde was completed A, B, & D batteries withdrawing their guns and ordnance to their wagon lines which were not taken over by the incoming brigade.
C battery went into action again under orders of the 172 Bde

29. A, B & D batteries marched to Calais training area
Billets for the night at MALLON CAPPELL

WAR DIARY
INTELLIGENCE SUMMARY

17th Bde R.F.A.

26-Jun

Place	Date	Hour	Summary of Events and Information	Remarks and references to Appendices
	30		The brigade (less C battery) marched to LUMBRES billeting for the night there.	
	31		The third stage of the march was originally intended to bring the brigade to the training area. Owing to this last march being a long one, was horses on NABRINGEN and COLEMBERT when the brigade billeted for the night. The necessary supply columns accompanying the brigade also a detachment of the R.A.M.C. [illegible]	

March to billets area

Hornsby at
for Lt Colonel
O.C. 17th Bde R.F.A

Appendix H

SECRET

Copy No. 10

SPANBROEK GROUP ORDER No. 2

1. A Bombardment of the enemys trenches opposite the 49th Infantry Brigade by Trench Mortars will take place on Wednesday 27th December at 2-15 p.m.

2. The Artillery will cooperate as under in order to keep under the fire of Enemy Trench Mortars and to engage enemys O.P's

Tasks for batteries as follows:-

C/173   Front line and high ground round SPANBROEK MOLEN including O.P's at :-
- N.30.a.15.03.
- N.30.c.45.40.
- N.30.c.35.70.
- N.30.c.40.80.

B/173   Trench from N.30.a.98.95. to N.30.a.70.22.

D/173   Trench Mortars at :-
- N.30.c.50.70.
- N.30.c.68.91.
- N.30.d.23.95.
- N.30.a.80.10.

3. Rates of fire

   ※ 18 pdr up to 1 round per gun per two minutes.

     4.5 Howitzer 1 round per gun per two minutes.

  ※ Note.   18 pdrs will start firing at the rate of 1 round per gun every 3 minutes. If the enemy retaliation is heavy the rate of fire will be increased at the descretion of Group Commanders for as long as he considers necessary up to but not exceeding 1 round per gun per 2 minutes.

4. The Bombardment will be carried out as follows:-

    2.15 p.m. — 2.45. p.m.   Bombardment

    2.45p.m. — 3.0p.m.   Interval But batteries on Trench Mortars may continue firing if these are active.

    3.0 p.m. — 3.30.p.m.   Bombardment.

5. Ammunition allowed will be

    18pdr. batteries   180 rounds per Battery

    4.5" Howitzer "   120 " " "

6. The Enemy Trench Mortars opposite the front of the 47th Infantry Brigade will be watched by A/173, x A/153 and D/153 batteries.

A/173 will at once engage any mortar which is active and will call upon the Group H.Q. for assistance if required.

x A list of T.M. positions opposite the 47th Infantry Brigade is forwarded.

Rates of fire and expenditure of ammunition will be controlled by Group H.Q. except that A/173 may fire 8 rounds at any trench mortar reported active without reference to Group H.Q.

7. Watches will be synchronised with Group H.Q. at 12.30p.m. on 27.12.16.

8. Acknowledge.

Lt. Col. R.F.A.
Commanding SPANBROEK GROUP R.F.A.

Issued at 12 noon
25.12.16.

Copies to :-

No.1.   16th D.A.
" 2.   47th Infy. Bde.
   3.   A/173
   4.   B/173
   5.   C/173
   6.   D/173
   7.   A/153
   8.   D/153
   9.   153rd Bde. H.Q.
  10.   War Diary
  11.   "
  12.   File

WAR DIARY.

173rd BRIGADE, R.F.A.

36th Division.

SECRET

173 BdeRHA Army Form C. 2118.
36 Div

WAR DIARY
or
INTELLIGENCE SUMMARY.
(Erase heading not required.)

Army Form C. 2118.

Instructions regarding War Diaries and Intelligence Summaries are contained in F. S. Regs., Part II. and the Staff Manual respectively. Title pages will be prepared in manuscript.

Place	Date	Hour	Summary of Events and Information	Remarks and references to Appendices
	JANUARY 1917			
	1		The Brigade, less C Battery, arrived in the Calais training area, and was billeted in the villages allotted as follows. A/173 in TARDINGHEN, LE CHATELAIT and MUSCONFUM	
			B/173 in AUDINGHEM	
			D/173 in FRAMZELLE	
			H.Q. in FRAMZELLE	
	2		The Field Ambulance attached to Bde in FRAMZELLE	
			ASC Supply train " " in AUDINGHEM	
			Parades under orders of Battery Commanders and checking of gun stores, equipment &c.	
	3,4,5,6		Battery training carried on daily	
	7		The MGRA Second Army (Major General Franks) visited Batteries	
	8		Batteries were visited by GOCRA 36 Div (Brig. Gen. H. Brook) Daily training carried out as usual	
	9th,10-11th		Battery training carried out daily	

WAR DIARY
or
INTELLIGENCE SUMMARY.
(Erase heading not required.)

Army Form C. 2118.

173 Bde R.F.A.
36th Div.

Ref: 1/100,000 Sheet 5.W.A. Belgium & Sheet 5.W. Belgium

Place	Date	Hour	Summary of Events and Information	Remarks and references to Appendices
	January 1917			
	12		Ref. 1/100,000 Ploegsteert. The Brigade less B & C Batteries commenced its march back to the Div. Area billeting for the night at ESCOEUILLES and QUESQUES. B. Battery remained in the training area going to an outbreak of mange.	Appx. 1
	13		March continued to CAMPAGNE and RACQUINGHEM	
	14		March continued to BORRE and PRADELLES	
	15		March continued to Wagon Lines. Starting from 5 p.m, the Brigade less A Battery & A.M.M. B. Battery relieved 172 Brigade less A Battery	Appx. B.2
NEUVE EGLISE	16		The Brigade became the RIGHT Group. O.C. 172 Brigade handed over to O.C. 173 Brigade at 7.30 p.m. at NEUVE EGLISE.	Appx. C.1
	17		A Bombardment of the enemy support line Communications was carried out from 4.50 - 5 p.m. No counter-Battery work was attempted by the enemy.	
	18		Lt.Col. H. C. Simpson D.S.O. R.F.A. took command of the Div. Artillery during the absence of Brig. Gen. H.J. Mack D.S.O. on leave. Major C.A. Reid Scott D.S.O. R.F.A. assumed command of the Brigade.	
	19		Artillery activity against T.11.d during the afternoon. Slight enemy Observation - N.I.	

WAR DIARY
or
INTELLIGENCE SUMMARY.
(Erase heading not required.)

Army Form C. 2118.

Instructions regarding War Diaries and Intelligence Summaries are contained in F. S. Regs., Part II. and the Staff Manual respectively. Title pages will be prepared in manuscript.

Place	Date	Hour	Summary of Events and Information	Remarks and references to Appendices
NEUVE EGLISE	January 1915 20th		Increased enemy artillery activity during the day. A/172 Battery position received about 30 15cm shells. At 12.25 p.m. the Boup Concentration "E" was carried out in response to a message from Infantry. An enemy T.M. (Iron) was active during the morning and was duly punished. There was also slight Artillery activity during the day.	
	21st		Was war flat. Enemy Artillery activity from 2 p.m. until about 7. Enemy T.M.s were also active. At 3.20 p.m. Concentration "E" was carried out and the signal of the Party. The enemy bombardment appeared to be directed chiefly at Mainly the front of the Division on our right. At about 5 p.m. S.O.S. signals were reported to have been up on our right. Gun right Battalion were on the line was out of communication with the companies in the front line sent through the S.O.S. but the signal fire immediately at about 6 p.m. in the gloom came appeared to be from	

WAR DIARY or INTELLIGENCE SUMMARY

Army Form C. 2118.

Place	Date	Hour	Summary of Events and Information	Remarks and references to Appendices
NEUVE EGLISE	22		right, our right Battery used 18 the assistance of the Boyd on our right. Our remains 2 @ 18 pdr Batteries covering the Boyd had sent the left of the left Boyd. At some time between 5 & 6 a.m. a small party of the enemy succeeded in closing on Trenches on an extreme right. It is possible that they came along from the flanks the real point of entry being on the front of the Division to our right. The attack all renewed on our line, for a short time and later area with them a 9" T.M. belonging to X/36 T.M. Battery run away with the time away to a faulty Rifle burster was out of action during the detachment had been withdrawn. Day very quiet. The casualties were remarkably small. Call 5 slight cases of wounded being reported from the 109th Infantry X/36 Dty R.S. 3 men wounded 2 of them being over 2000 rounds of ammunition were fired by the Right Boyd between 7 hrs. & 9 a.m. During the afternoon the enemy heard bombarded our Trenches with tear shell air without effect.	

WAR DIARY or INTELLIGENCE SUMMARY

Army Form C. 2118.

Place	Date	Hour	Summary of Events and Information	Remarks and references to Appendices
Neuve Eglise	Jan 23		A quiet day with some enemy aerial activity during and early afternoon.	
	24		Frosty weather continues. Observation very good. No enemy aircraft. Patrols at work during the day.	
	25		At intervals during the day the enemy shelled B.11.2 Dutton posts at T.17.a.46.22. About 300 10's [shells] were fired about entirely H.E. The enemy had the long hospital and numerous rounds fell between the guns. One direct hit was obtained on the Dugline Pit which set and wrecked the gun pit. Our gunner twice and wrecked the gun carriage but damaged beyond repair x Knife & breech were safe. One day adv all day. Allowed hostile observation. Cordite was extend post for direction.	x There were no casualties to personnel although the shelling was heavy & the shell dump was hit. Ale shelling was very
	26		Hostile artillery was again extremely active especially on the Dutton trench field line at T.16.d and T.22.b were heavily shelled at 10.15 and 15 cm Austrian. One fuse was dislodged at ...	

WAR DIARY
or
INTELLIGENCE SUMMARY.
(Erase heading not required.)

Army Form C. 2118.

Instructions regarding War Diaries and Intelligence Summaries are contained in F.S. Regs., Part II. and the Staff Manual respectively. Title pages will be prepared in manuscript.

Place	Date	Hour	Summary of Events and Information	Remarks and references to Appendices
NEUVE EGLISE	Jan. 1917 26		We use a few slight casualties and observation fair.	
ENGLISH FARM	27		Regt. from H.Q. moved to ENGLISH FARM T 21 d 21. Enemy Artillery less active but enemy aircraft closed our lines especially. A good deal of sub-was done by us today in connection with the Defence of the Line and especially of Hill 63 Reserve Switch Line Def. of Batteries and T.M.s. We reconnoitred and the situation discussed and explained at a Conference of Battery Commanders. Re Counter enemy Artillery and devil assault and to systematic enemy agitation related by the Infantry leads to the belief that the enemy is planning some offensive before a thaw sets in. Enemy Aircraft still very active especially machines of the Albatross Type. Enemy Artillery less active. Our Artillery stood a policy of retaliation and wire cutting: actual bombardments being avoided.	
	28			

Enemy Aircraft was also very active.

WAR DIARY or INTELLIGENCE SUMMARY

Army Form C. 2118.

Place	Date	Hour	Summary of Events and Information	Remarks and references to Appendices
	January 1917			
ENGLISH FARM	29		Enemy aircraft very active and dropped about twenty or thirty bombs. Machine crossed our lines and remained out. Item for nearly an hour. Our anti-aircraft fire was ineffective. Observation posts active. Enemy batteries.	
	30		Our batteries continued to register various targets and to cut wire. No activity by enemy artillery.	
	31		During the afternoon DINK Valley [trench] North at T.18.d.0.0 was subjected to a heavy bombardment by 15 cm howitzer. Heat damage was done and all telephone lines were destroyed. One gun was put out of action (No. 1). On being demolished altogether the fire they interchanged. Casualties: 1 O.R. killed, 1 Officer & 6 O.R. wounded. We called up Battalion and bombarded 18 selected points. Were carried out. An artillery battle of 15 cm bosche battery was located and shell all 2 our heavy counter battery.	

Ed. Jeaticeck Major R.F.A.
Commanding 173 Bde. R.F.A.

SECRET   Copy No.

36TH DIVISIONAL ARTILLERY ORDER NO 48

1. Consequent on the reorganisation of the Divisional Artillery the following moves and reliefs will take place.

2. On the 13th instant one Section D/172nd Bde. R.F.A. will be transferred complete to D/153rd Bde. R.F.A. and be absorbed. At the same time the gun detachments of the Section C/172nd Bde. R.F.A. attached to D/153rd Bde. R.F.A. will be transferred to position occupied by remaining Section of D/172nd Bde. R.F.A.

3. On the nights of 15th and 16th instants 173rd Bde. R.F.A. less "B" Battery will relieve 172nd Bde. R.F.A. less "A" Battery in action, in accordance with attached Table.

4. No move will take place before 5 p.m. and incoming Batteries will not arrive on positions before that time on either day.

5. All Trench Stores, Maps, Registrations, etc, will be handed over by outgoing Units.

6. Command of Right Group will pass at 172nd Brigade H.Q. at 7.30 p.m. 16th January 1917.

7. Completion of reliefs to be wired to R.A.H.Q. in code.

8. Separate orders as to changes in Wagon Lines, consequent on reorganisation are being issued.

9. ACKNOWLEDGE.

Issued at 7.0. a.m.   (sd) H.D.Gale
11.1.17.   Major, R.F.A.
                              A/Brigade Major, 36th Divl. Artillery.

C1

PROGRAMME OF BOMBARDMENT

UNIT	No. of GUNS	TASK	AMMUNITION
A/173	5 guns	ULCER SUPPORT U8b 28.71-U2d 43.20.	150 A.X.
	1 gun	Communication Trench U8b 04.57- U8b 28.71.	30 A.
A/172	6 guns	ULCER SUPPORT U2d 43.20.- U2b 45.04.	180 A.X.
C/173	3 guns	BETHLEHEM FARM U3d 50.65.	90 A.X.
	3 guns	SCHNITZEL FARM U3c 80.15.	90 A.X.
D/173	1 gun	U8a 95.70)	
	1 "	U8b 28.71.)	
	1 "	U2c 90.65)	
	1 "	U2b 45.04.)	
	1 "	U2c 85.95)	
	1 "	U2b 80.30.)	120 B.X.

SECRET   C1   Copy No.

RIGHT GROUP ORDER No 1.

1. A Bombardment of hostile support line and communications will be carried out on 17th inst on the occasion of a probable infantry relief.

2. The zero time will be 4.50. p.m.

3. Rates of fire :-

      18 pdrs   3 rounds per gun per minute
      4.5" How   2   "   "   "   "   "

4. Duration of bombardment 10 minutes

5. Batteries will fire as per attached programme

6. Watches will be synchronized with Group Headquarters at 3.35. p.m.

7. Acknowledge by wire.

H.C. Pip.

17.1.17.   Lt. Col. R.F.A.
Commanding Right Group R.F.A.
36th Divl. Arty.

for information.

Issued at

Copy No. 1. to A/173
     2. A/172
     3. C/173
     4. D/173
     5. 109 Infy Bde *for information*
     6. 36th Div Arty.
     7. War Diary
     8. File

Vol 16

WAR DIARY

173rd BDE. R.F.A.
36th DIVISION.

WAR DIARY
INTELLIGENCE SUMMARY.
(Erase heading not required.)

173rd Brigade R.F.A.   36th Div.

Army Form C. 2118.

Place	Date	Hour	Summary of Events and Information	Remarks and references to Appendices
ENGLISH FARM	February 1917			
	1		Ref. 28 S.W. 4 Edition 4A 1/10,000 PLOEGSTEERT. Enemy continued to devote attention to Counter Battery work. D/173 position at T.18.d. o. r. was again shelled heavily with 15 c.m. & 10.5 c.m. Further casualties were sustained × and the position rendered untenable. During the night the Battery moved to a new position at T.24.d.9.4.	× Total casualties during 2 days Bombardment Killed O.R. 3 Died of wounds 1 Wounded O.R. 8 " Officer 1
	2		Hostile Artillery was fairly active, especially on back areas. Observation was exceptionally good. Hostile Aircraft took every advantage of it, 9 machines practically all of the Albatross type being reported by an Observer to have 'crossed' our lines. Our Artillery was also active and some reputation was carried out with Aeroplane co-operation.	
	3		Hostile Artillery was less active. he carried out the usual agitation wire cutting.	
	4		A fire broke out in the Brigade office which was entirely destroyed. A lot of valuable property was destroyed but most of the Brigade Records were saved.	
	5		A wire-cutting operation lasting for one hour was carried out during the afternoon. Trench mortars cooperated. Owing to very poor visibility the wire-cutting was not as successful as it might have been	

Army Form C. 2118.

WAR DIARY
or
INTELLIGENCE SUMMARY.
(Erase heading not required.)

Place	Date	Hour	Summary of Events and Information	Remarks and references to Appendices
ENGLISH FARM	February 1917			
	5		Enemy retaliation was slight except for a shot bombardment on our left subsector to which we replied by firing a few rounds on communication trenches.	APP A
	6		Hostile Artillery & Aircraft Considerably less active. Observation poor.	
	7		Hostile aircraft active. Otherwise nothing of note.	
	8		Gun Artillery & Trench Mortar fire rained at were rained at by our artillery and	
	9		At 12 noon a bombardment was rained at by our artillery and Medium & Heavy T.M's. No states broken also co-operated. Much damage is reported to have been done.	APP B
	10		The enemy was observed in several places repairing the damage done by yesterday's bombardment. Our own programme of wire cutting was carried out. Enemy Artillery is showing much less activity. Hostile aircraft continue to cross our lines frequently.	
	11		A "Sylt" flare set in lit by the enemy it was freezing. again. At 9.47 a.m. a train was loaded to take MESSINES. A pre-arranged bombardment of suspected dump Railway terminus in O 32 d was rained at. Our guns were active throughout	

Army Form C. 2118.

WAR DIARY
or
INTELLIGENCE SUMMARY.
(Erase heading not required.)

Instructions regarding War Diaries and Intelligence Summaries are contained in F. S. Regs., Part II. and the Staff Manual respectively. Title pages will be prepared in manuscript.

Place	Date	Hour	Summary of Events and Information	Remarks and references to Appendices
	11		The day passed in daily wire cutting tasks, destructive bombardments and harassing concentrations	
	12		Observation was very bad. Consequently Artillery on both sides were considerably less active. 2" T.M's cut wire effectively.	
	13		Visibility again low. Enemy trench mortars showed slight activity during the afternoon. 2" T.M.s again cut wire.	Lt. A. C. Simpson DSO RFA resumed command of the Brigade
	14		A certain amount of hostile work and movement was observed. Hostile artillery was fairly active and fired at aeroplane observation.	
	15		Weather much warmer and visibility good. Hostile Artillery	
	16		Quiet. An enemy T.M. was repeatedly active. Silenced by our 4.5" Hows. A hostile aeroplane was brought down by A.A. fire at the Rgt. captured. The thaw started. Our planes show much fresh activity and	
	17		the enemy aircraft correspondingly less. Enemy artillery fairly active. During the morning a bombardment was carried out in support of a minor operation carried out by the Division on our Right. Enemy retaliated heavily on the right of our front.	App. C

WAR DIARY
or
INTELLIGENCE SUMMARY.
(Erase heading not required.)

Army Form C. 2118.

Place	Date	Hour	Summary of Events and Information	Remarks and references to Appendices
ENGLISH FARM	February 18		Enemy artillery active - four front concentrations were fired at the expected Inf. Infantry. Working parties were observed during the day behind the enemy line.	
	19		Quiet unit all day. Operations.	APP D
	20		Quiet and wet. Flgl. Trench Mortar activity on the part of the enemy duly humbled by our Artillery. Otherwise quiet. Lieut Col H.C. SIMPSON D.S.O. R.F.A. proceeded on leave. Command of the four being taken over by Major G.R.O. EDWARDS D.S.O. R.F.A.	
	21		During the evening a minor operation was carried out by the 104th Brigade. Enemy trenches were entered but found to be unoccupied.	App. DE
	22		and full of fine. Enemy retreated ineffectively to on A/172 at T17a4622. A, B, + C Battery Wagon Lines moved from DRANOUTRE to PENZANCE LINES, WELLINGTON LINES and NEWCOMBE FARM respectively. During this and the following night B/173 out relieved A/172 at T17a4622 with a detached section at T17d52.	
	23		During the early morning a small party of the enemy attempted	

Army Form C. 2118.

WAR DIARY
or
INTELLIGENCE SUMMARY.
(Erase heading not required.)

Instructions regarding War Diaries and Intelligence Summaries are contained in F. S. Regs., Part II. and the Staff Manual respectively. Title pages will be prepared in manuscript.

Place	Date	Hour	Summary of Events and Information	Remarks and references to Appendices
ENGLISH FARM	Feb. 1917			
	23		to enter our lines near ANTON'S FARM but was driven back by M.G. fire. At the same time the enemy raided the Division on our right.	
	24		Operations nil.	
	25		Observation impossible owing to mist. Situation quiet.	
	26		Owing to faulty food weather conditions artillery on both sides was more active. One hostile plane appeared over our lines	
	27		Lieut Col H.C. Simpson D.S.O. R.F.A. returned from leave and resumed command of the group.	
	27		Enemy Artillery fairly active, in spite of mist.	
	28		Nothing unusual occurred	

H.C.S.
Lieut Col R.F.A.
Commanding Right Group.

WAR DIARY
or
INTELLIGENCE SUMMARY.
(Erase heading not required.)

Army Form C. 2118.

173rd Brigade R.F.A.
36th Div. IX Corps 2nd Army

Vol 17

Place	Date	Hour	Summary of Events and Information	Remarks and references to Appendices
ENGLISH FARM	March 1917		Reference Maps: (1) Sheet 28 S.W.4. PLOEGSTEERT 1:10000 Ed.4A (2) Sheet 28 S.W. 1:20000 Ed.3D	

Location of Units

Unit	Location	Wagon Line
Brigade H.Q	T 21 d 21	T 21 d 21
A Battery	T 23 b 4662	T 20 d 38
B Battery	T 17 a 4626	T 36 b 55 (detached section at T17d 54.12)
C Battery	T 24 a 2005	T 38 b 49
D Battery	T 24 d 9540	S 5 a 55

The Brigade, together with V/36 Heavy T.M Battery and X/36 Medium T.M Battery (on relieving Battery when X/36 is not in the line) forms the Right Group, 36th Div.

The Brigade Commander and Battery Commanders are as follows:

Brigade Commander — Lieut-Col H.C. SIMPSON D.S.O. R.F.A.
Adjutant — Lt- F.N BROOME R F A
Orderly Officer — Lieut H M ACHILLES R F A

Army Form C. 2118.

WAR DIARY
or
INTELLIGENCE SUMMARY.
(Erase heading not required.)

Instructions regarding War Diaries and Intelligence Summaries are contained in F. S. Regs., Part II. and the Staff Manual respectively. Title pages will be prepared in manuscript.

Place	Date	Hour	Summary of Events and Information	Remarks and references to Appendices
ENGLISH FARM	March 1917			
			A Battery	
			Major C.A.L Brownlow R.F.A.	
			Capt. A Ruddy R.F.A (Second in Command)	
			B. Battery	
			Major A H Burne D.S.O R.F.A	
			Capt. H R G. Guinness R.F.A (Second in Command)	
			C Battery	
			Major G.R.O. Edwards D.S.O R.F.A	
			Capt. G.A Rickards R.F.A (Second in Command)	
			D Battery	
			Major C.A Reid Scott D.S.O. R.F.A	
			Capt. C.L. Chapman M.C R.F.A (Second in Command)	

WAR DIARY or INTELLIGENCE SUMMARY

Army Form C. 2118.

Place	Date	Hour	Summary of Events and Information	Remarks and references to Appendices
	March 1917			
	1.		Owing probably to exceptionally bad weather conditions enemy artillery was fairly active chiefly against back areas. A Battery of the left group in T.16.a. was heavily shelled, causing casualties and considerable material damage. The enemy sent up a number of Observation Balloons and unsuccessfully attacked one of ours. From 7 p.m. until 6 a.m. the following day the group carried on an intermittent bombardment of the enemy lines.	
	2.		Hostile Artillery again active. Many hours behind our lines were sprayed with Shrapnel and B/ Battery detached section was deliberately shelled. 3 men were wounded, one gun was subsequently died and a cook house was destroyed.	App. A
	3.		Artillery was inactive on both sides. The M.G.R.A. 2nd Army visited Battery positions.	
	4.		Enemy 77 m/m guns & 10.5 cm hows. were active against various points. A number of 10.5 cm hows. shells burst on or near the RED LODGE Road in T.18.d. An enemy T.M. also fired until silenced by artillery. Lieut Col H. E. Simpson D.S.O. J.R.F.A. proceeded to 2nd Army H.Q. on duty. Major G.R.O. EDWARDS D.S.O. R.F.A. assumed command of the Brigade.	

Army Form C. 2118.

WAR DIARY
or
INTELLIGENCE SUMMARY.
(Erase heading not required.)

Instructions regarding War Diaries and Intelligence Summaries are contained in F. S. Regs, Part II. and the Staff Manual respectively. Title pages will be prepared in manuscript.

Place	Date	Hour	Summary of Events and Information	Remarks and references to Appendices
ENGLISH FARM	March 1917			
	5		Very misty all day. Situation normal.	
	6		A, B & D Batteries cooperated with the left group in a bombardment of the enemy communication Trenches. Enemy retaliation was weak. During the bombardment an enemy aeroplane descended within a few feet of our Trenches.	APP B
	7		A bombardment of enemy trenches was carried out again. Enemy retaliation was weak.	APP C
	8		No event of importance occurred	
	9		B Battery was again heavily shelled during the morning with 15 cm howitzer shells. A direct hit was obtained on the telephone pit which withstood the shock. An dugout was lit during January. No damage done. Casualties to personnel, 1 O.R. wounded (slight). A great deal of movement behind the enemy lines was observed, due, indeed, to exceptionally fine food in hills.	
	10		Quiet day. Award revealed decoration. Lieut Col. H.C. SIMPSON D.S.O. R.F.A. assumed command of the Group	

Army Form C. 2118.

WAR DIARY
or
INTELLIGENCE SUMMARY.
(Erase heading not required.)

Instructions regarding War Diaries and Intelligence Summaries are contained in F. S. Regs., Part II. and the Staff Manual respectively. Title pages will be prepared in manuscript.

Place	Date	Hour	Summary of Events and Information	Remarks and references to Appendices
	March 1917			
	11		Moderate Artillery activity. A Battery of the left group in T.16.d was heavily hit 10.15 & 15 c.m. Hostile aircraft very active in the afternoon. 2 hostile planes attacked an observation balloon near NIEPPE and destroyed it. The observers escaped by parachute.	
	12, 13		Moderate enemy artillery activity.	
	14		At 12 noon the Right Group ceased to exist as a tactical unit, A, C & D Batteries being attached tactically to the Group on the Right, and B Battery to the Group on the Left.	
	15		Situation normal	
	16		The Relief of the Right Group by the Left Group New Zealand Div. Artillery began. The Brigade on relief relieved its left group 161st Div. Artillery forming together with A/150, C/153 and D/153 the SPANBROEK GROUP, covering the 107th Infantry Brigade.	App. D
ENGLISH FARM	17		The above relief was completed. Hqrs. were located as follows:-	

Army Form C. 2118.

WAR DIARY
or
INTELLIGENCE SUMMARY

(Erase heading not required.)

Place	Date	Hour	Summary of Events and Information	Remarks and references to Appendices
LITTLE KEMMEL	March 1917			
	17		Unit Location Name (Major Lines) Location	
			Group H.Q. N20d 84	
			A/173 (1 Section) N33 a 81 ACKWORTH LINES M35 d 85	
			(2 Sections) T24 a 28 PENZANCE LINES T20 d 38	
			B/173 N26 d 70 NORBURY LINES S5 b 36	
			C/173 N3 a 88 DURBAN LINES S5 b 83	
			D/173 N27 a 13 WOBURN LINES S5 a 55	
			A/153 N15 b 35 85 AYRSHIRE LINES M35 d 44	
			C/153 N15 d 22 RUDDIGORE FARM M28 d 11	
			D/153 N26 8075 MUDVEEW LINES M34 d 98	
	18		Quiet: Nothing unusual occurred.	

Army Form C. 2118.

WAR DIARY
or
INTELLIGENCE SUMMARY
(Erase heading not required.)

Place	Date	Hour	Summary of Events and Information	Remarks and references to Appendices
LITTLE KEMMEL	March 1917 19, 20		Only normal activity. During the night the Battery of 153rd Brigade attached to the Bgde were withdrawn from action, and the position of the remaining Batteries altered accordingly, so as to cover the same front front.	App E
	21, 22, 23		Visibility exceptionally good. A great deal of railway traffic was observed behind the enemy lines was fairly active with T.M's, also shelling our back areas.	
	24		Between 4 and 5 a.m. after a heavy bombardment the enemy attempted a raid on our front. He attempted to enter our line on our extreme right but our fire is reported to have caught him in his left in trenches stores him back. Lewis gun fire was also said to be very effective. Gun Batteries were firing from 4.3 a.m. to 5.16 a.m. Ammunition expended: 1022 A 521 AX 152 BX. No 2 Battalion Relieg the line report about 30 casualties. A Battery layer Sun moved from PENZANCE LINES to BURNE LINES (S.5.d 88)	
	25		Nothing unusual occurred	

2449 Wt. W14957/M90 750,000 1/16 J.B.C. & A. Forms/C.2118/12.

Army Form C. 2118.

WAR DIARY
or
INTELLIGENCE SUMMARY

(Erase heading not required.)

Place	Date	Hour	Summary of Events and Information	Remarks and references to Appendices
LITTLE KEMMEL	March 1917			
	26th		Lieut-Col H.C. Simpson D.S.O. R.F.A. proceeded to the Polincove Training Area to reconnoitre a scheme of training for the Brigade. Major G.R.O. Edwards D.S.O. R.F.A. assumed command of the Brigade during his absence.	
	27th		Artillery unusual	
	28th		Lieut-Col H.C. Simpson D.S.O. R.F.A. resumed command of the Group.	
	29th 30th 31st		Normal Trench Warfare. Enemy artillery active at T24b & 28 & was heavily shelled during the morning. Some damage done.	

H.C. Simpson
Lieut Col. R.F.A.
Commanding 173 Brigade R.F.A.

Army Form C. 2118.

WAR DIARY
or
INTELLIGENCE SUMMARY

(Erase heading not required.)

173rd Brigade R.F.A. 36th Div IX Corps

Place	Date	Hour	Summary of Events and Information	Remarks and references to Appendices
April	1	1917	Quiet day; very misty.	Second Army
	2		Quiet; occasional shootings interfered with observation.	
	3		An exceptionally clear day. A good amount of movement was observed behind the enemy lines. The enemy has started putting up a smoke barrage behind his lines in order to interfere with our observation.	
	4		Very quiet.	
	5		A battle plane was brought down by an FE8, landing near DRANOUTRE. The pilot was slightly wounded. During the evening an enterprise was carried out by the Division on our left. No fewer than four group bombardments by the 87th Brigade R.F.A. co-operated. There were heavy bombardments on the 2 day however, to the raid, on to day of the raid itself. Enemy trenches near PECKHAM were raided & 21 prisoners secured. Our casualties reported slight. Confused with its number engaged (one Battalion). Enemy retaliation was heavy on our trenches. Various points near LINDENHOEK were also shelled.	Appx. A
	6		Quiet.	
	7		153 Brigade R.F.A. returned from its Training Area; 3 of their Batteries	

WAR DIARY
or
INTELLIGENCE SUMMARY

(Erase heading not required.)

Army Form C. 2118.

Place	Date	Hour	Summary of Events and Information	Remarks and references to Appendices
	8		enforcing the fronts. During the afternoon and while the relief was taking place, the enemy shelled the position at N13 b 43 & copied by a section of C/178. Several casualties were caused among the personnel of C/153 the guns one to the position taken over and considerable damage was done. It was decided to evacuate the position consequently A/153 did not go into action. During the night a hostile aeroplane dropped bombs near KEMMEL and fired on troops on the LINDENHOEK - NEUVE EGLISE road causing one casualty to A Battery. No night was clear + moonlit. Hostile artillery activity during the day. C Battery in action.	App. B
	9		At N33 a 88 was heavily shelled. Lt no Casualties were caused. Lt. SIMMONDS was cut in the neck by a fragment of glass from a window. Various other points were shelled here also. Enemy shell concentration. Enemy artillery inactive. Our Batteries fired numerous concentrations on enemy points. Over 900 rounds were expended on 2nd Concentration.	
	10		Windy weather, with occasional snow storm during the day. Front quiet.	
	11		Our artillery carried out a number of concentrations	

Army Form C. 2118.

WAR DIARY
or
INTELLIGENCE SUMMARY
(Erase heading not required.)

Instructions regarding War Diaries and Intelligence Summaries are contained in F.S. Regs., Part II. and the Staff Manual respectively. Title Pages will be prepared in manuscript.

Place	Date	Hour	Summary of Events and Information	Remarks and references to Appendices
LITTLE KEMMEL	April	12	Quiet: visibility poor. Took on MAGNUM OPUS portions proceeded, each Battery supplying a working party of 30 men in addition to those working on their own portions. It is intended to provide one shop concealed dugout for each portion and also 3 dugouts with at concrete. Ammunition dumps and recesses to be splinter and weather proof, and gun teamsters tools in pits under Camouflage.	
		13	Considerable activity of hostile Aircraft and Artillery; visibility good. Station normal.	
		14		
		15-19	Nothing unusual. Rain and wet weather prevented good observation and hindered operations. The attitude of the enemy has been quiet, and all our efforts to force his Artillery have been unsuccessful.	
		2.15	At about 4.30 p.m. a man of the 2nd Prussian Division came over to our lines opposite SPANBROEKMOLEN. He stated that the enemy Trenches were badly flooded and much damaged by our fire, that rations had been reduced and that the morale of the Division was very low indeed. He offered that time and induce some of his friends to desert. He left our front line was frightened by machine gun fire. Do returned to our trenches without having reached the enemy lines. The prisoner confirmed that a raid is taking place that night.	

2449 Wt. W14957/M90 750,000 1/16 J.B.C. & A. Forms/C.2118/12.

Army Form C. 2118.

WAR DIARY
or
INTELLIGENCE SUMMARY

(Erase heading not required.)

Place	Date	Hour	Summary of Events and Information	Remarks and references to Appendices
LITTLE KEMMEL	April 20th		Angell Group was twice carried out by the Group, the heavy artillery co-operating on Oak Grove. A bombardment was also carried out during the day. App III C & D	
	21st		Enemy remained quiet.	
	22,23,24		Clear fine weather. Situation normal. The front held by the 36th Division extends from (inclusive) the WULVERGHEM - WYTSCHAETE Road to MAEDELSTEDE FARM. One Brigade of Infantry is in the line supported by one Group of Field Artillery known as the SPANBROEK GROUP. This Group consists of 6 six-gun 18 pdr Batteries and 2 six-gun 4.5 howitzer Batteries. Of these 4 18 pdr Batteries and one 18 pdr Section and one 4.5 how:r Battery are actually firing, the remainder being "in action but not i.e. they do not man O.P's nor Cover Patrols Companies May have Reserve S.O.S. points allotted to them, and in the event of an enemy attack would be called on to reinforce the Barrage. No method of dealing with enemy T.M. and other activity has proved very successful. Very heavy enemy T.M. is given a barrage in return sent to from as one of them in reply to active barrage on those June the T.M. is put in Headquarters. The 18 pdr Battery in whose Zone the T.M. is found also the 4.5 how:r Battery deal with it. New	

WAR DIARY
or
INTELLIGENCE SUMMARY

Army Form C. 2118.

Place	Date	Hour	Summary of Events and Information	Remarks and references to Appendices
LITTLE KEMMEL	April 1917		also a system of fresh concentrations to deal with every Battery fire on (b) general harass of enemy gates. Guns were enabled, after the flash plan concentrations each known by a distinct letter, are of place to respond at a moment's notice to call — all Batteries on placed "Concentration A", 5 rounds gun fire, upon which each Batt all Batteries have repeated until the order "Halt" was given the order. Fire a slow from front HQ to "Halt" Batteries simultaneous. As many as 10 rounds per gun have been fired. According to information received from the Seaforths who relieved us here. Concentrations are much pleasanter to the enemy By prompt dealing with even the slightest attempt on the part of the enemy to have succeeded in relieving our T.M. has been kept permanent inactive fire in general for 3 L.T. mortars of the other Bn. Concentrations & given and with full plenty fire comes as a salvo from 24 guns, its "Lethal" of power burst in 6th front, effective	
	24		Lt Col Stratton D.S.O. P.A.C. proceeded to Paris on 6 days leave during his absence the part was commanded by Lt Col R.B. Thomson D.S.O. P.O.	

WAR DIARY or INTELLIGENCE SUMMARY

Army Form C. 2118.

(Erase heading not required.)

Place	Date	Hour	Summary of Events and Information	Remarks and references to Appendices
LITTLE KEMMEL	24		The Brigade being commanded by Major A.H. BORNE DSO R.F.A.	
	25/4		Enemy Trench Mortars & Artillery more lively (than was usual)	
	26/4		Unusual	
	27/4		Considerable Trench Mortar activity during the day. The enemy's trench line is very much altered.	
	28/4 29/4 30/4		The Prussians left this part of the line. Nothing unusual occurred	

Reference (a) Trench Map WYTSCHAETE 28 S.W. 2 Edition 4 A
Scale 1: 10,000

(b) France Sheet 28 S.W. Edition 4 A
Scale 1: 20,000

J.H. Pitt
Commanding 173 Brigade R.F.A.

WAR DIARY or INTELLIGENCE SUMMARY

Army Form C. 2118.

173rd Brigade R.F.A.
36th Div. IX Corps
Second Army

Place	Date	Hour	Summary of Events and Information	Remarks and references to Appendices
	May 1917		Reg. Inst. FRANCE Sheet 28 SW Edition 5A	
	1		During the night 30th April to 1st May a bombardment of the enemy communication trenches was carried out, as it was suspected that App A. relief was taking place. At midnight a heavy barrage was opened on the STANDBOEKMOLEN Salient. The App A & B raiders the enemy trenches in front of the salient. Not much was effected. The enemy had, as soon as they saw our bombardment, evacuated outpost garrisons & had on the own artillery and heavy M.G. concentration was laid on some new well selected line which is believed to be the reserve line. Our intermittent fire was also maintained. Trench mortars and artillery attempts were made to put up a barrage. Capt. Kenyon R.G.A. was wounded. Lieut. Col. H.C. Simpson D.S.O. R.F.A. F. in Command of the raid.	
	2		Weather mostly fine and clear. Hostile artillery fairly quiet. Some	
LITTLE KEMMEL	3, 4		enemy T.M. activity on the 4th. Gun activity normal. The enemy is making increasing use of smoke barrages behind his lines to interfere with our Counts Battery work.	
	5		At intervals throughout the night the enemy carried out determined bombardments of back areas on a wide front LA CLYTTE, NEUVE EGLISE, KEMMEL and various Camps. BUGS and roads received particular attention.	

WAR DIARY
or
INTELLIGENCE SUMMARY

Army Form C. 2118.

(Erase heading not required.)

Instructions regarding War Diaries and Intelligence Summaries are contained in F.S. Regs., Part II. and the Staff Manual respectively. Title Pages will be prepared in manuscript.

Place	Date	Hour	Summary of Events and Information	Remarks and references to Appendices
LITTLE KEMMEL	May 5	5	77 mm & 100 m.m. guns and 10.5 cm & 15 cm howitzer took part. During the night the enemy gun bombarded back areas in a very determined manner. His object appears to be to hinder our work which we are carrying on in connection with offensive operations with a view to putting a stop to the enemy night firing.	App. C.
		6	every gun position (except 12") in the Second Army area carried out 3 intense bombardments of enemy trenches, communications and back areas, of 5 minutes each, at 8.45 p.m. and 11 p.m. At about 9.30 p.m. the enemy attempted some retaliation but was immediately silenced. The programme for 18 pdrs and 4.5 howitzers was repeated twice during the night in addition to the above. The Divisional Artillery has been detailed to cooperate in the task of neutralising hostile batteries.	
		8	At 11.10 p.m. the enemy opened a heavy bombardment on our trenches. Apparently a raid was intended, but it did not materialise.	
		9, 10	Quiet.	

Army Form C. 2118.

WAR DIARY
or
INTELLIGENCE SUMMARY
(Erase heading not required.)

Place	Date	Hour	Summary of Events and Information	Remarks and references to Appendices
LITTLE KEMMEL	May 1917 11		During the early morning the enemy bombarded a Baker parlour at N38a81. ~~The staff of the~~ One gun was completely wrecked and one man killed. The enemy counter battery work is very persistent. Ammunition is now being brought up for the MAGNUM OPUS.	
		12	About 10,000 rounds are sent up every night and placed in new positions in Shelter accommodation is available. Small preparations of night firing and wire-cutting are also being carried out. Using Ste Coryonction of the front wire-cutting is unusually found on this front except from line wire is invisible, except in a few places, and even front line wire can only be seen from KEMMEL. Much of the wire-cutting will have to be done to cut Caughane obstruction and will hardly ever using instantaneous fuze.	

Army Form C. 2118.

WAR DIARY
or
INTELLIGENCE SUMMARY

(Erase heading not required.)

Place	Date	Hour	Summary of Events and Information	Remarks and references to Appendices
LITTLE KEMMEL	May 1917	12, 13, 14, 15	Nothing unusual. A Battery at N33a 88 was heavily shelled in the early morning. One dugout was lit and damaged, and one man killed.	
		16 to 26	Enemy artillery activity has fractionally increased following a corresponding increase of our own. The enemy appear to be bringing up field artillery, especially 77 m.m. guns. 8.21 cm. howitzers have also appeared, and 10.5 cm. guns.	
		27	The 84th, 282nd, 161st, 168th, 108th and 76th Brigades R.F.A. moved up to positions which had been previously prepared for them. These the 161st & 168th Brigades belong to the 32nd Division where as the remainder are Army Field Brigades are in reserve. All the Brigades (including the 36th Div Artillery) and one grouped under the Artillery orders of the 36th Div Artillery, and are grouped as follows:	

Army Form C. 2118.

WAR DIARY
or
INTELLIGENCE SUMMARY
(Erase heading not required.)

Place	Date	Hour	Summary of Events and Information	Remarks and references to Appendices
N.35.6.81	May 27th		Right Group (Lt. Col. H.C. SIMPSON D.S.O. R.F.A.) 113th Brigade 84th Brigade 282nd Brigade 141st Brigade (attached) Each Group is subdivided into 2 sub groups. Right Group Head Quarters moved from LITTLE KEMMEL to the Advanced Divisional Head Quarters on KEMMEL HILL. During the past week the enemy has made repeated attempts to enter our Trenches and obtain identifications. Something like 9 or 3 attempts during one night and his raiding parties have been met by our fire and no success and several times our own Ranger	Left Group (Lt. Col. R.G. HONSOM D.S.O. R.F.A.) 153rd Brigade 108th " 76th " 168th " (attached)

WAR DIARY
INTELLIGENCE SUMMARY

Army Form C. 2118.

Place	Date	Hour	Summary of Events and Information	Remarks and references to Appendices
N26d81	May 27		Our raid on the 9th and have been successful for the most part though apparently the enemy line had been entered whilst our patrols and our parties had returned empty handed.	
	28		During the night the enemy persistently shelled back areas especially DRANOUTRE. Some much damage was done and many casualties caused to men and animals. Divisional Headquarters was rendered untenable and its O.R.E. killed. Divisional and R.E. Headquarters accordingly moved to their advanced Headquarters and the troop was ordered to occupy a divisional Battery position at N26d07.	
N21d07	29		Heavy shelling of back areas was again carried out by its enemy during the night with 15 and 10.5 cm. guns. In many cases it has been found necessary to evacuate sites lines straight. DRANOUTRE, LOCRE, CROIX DE POPERINGHE ST JANS CAPPEL, BAILLEUL and many other places were systematically bombarded. Also shelled areas which in fall	

WAR DIARY or INTELLIGENCE SUMMARY

Army Form C. 2118.

Place	Date	Hour	Summary of Events and Information	Remarks and references to Appendices
N26d07	May 29		be used to bivouac troops on were Bivouacked in accordance with the policy laid down in the enemy's sen last orders.	
	30		The enemy's counter battery work has increased and of the Combardment of roads back areas & Dim centres. No Supply of ammunition has been rendered much more difficult, especially to the horizons which can only be approached well after dark.	
	31		Usual night activity on the part of the enemy. Our artillery active throughout the day.	

J.E.B.
Lieut Col R.F.A.
Commanding 173 Bde R.F.A.

WAR DIARY or INTELLIGENCE SUMMARY

Army Form C. 2118.

173 Brigade R.F.A. Second Army
36th Div. IX Corps
Ref. Map: France Sheet 28 S.W. 1:20,000 28 S.A.

Place	Date	Hour	Summary of Events and Information	Remarks and references to Appendices
N26c90	June 1		Systematic bombardment of the enemy's trenches and back areas continued. During the day one was cut by 18 pdrs while 4.5 howitzer carried out deliberate destructive shoots on enemy trenches. Battery Position were filled up to complete establishment of ammunition. Of the 24 Battery Positions in the Group, 4 held 9000 rounds, 1 7800 rounds and 7 6600 rounds. In addition to this various natures of lethal and lachrimatory shell were issued to 4.5 howitzers and smoke shell to 18 pdrs. The enemy's activity was principally directed against back areas. He appears to have a number of High Velocity guns and areas as far back as BAILLEUL have come under fire. Much damage has been done to DRANOUTRE and Battery Wagon lines in the district.	
	2		A concentrated bombardment on MESSINES was carried out by the II ANZAC Heavy Artillery. Practice Ranges were also fired. The enemy's Counter Battery been lively, but very little damage was done to Batteries of the Group. Some ammunition was destroyed.	

Army Form C. 2118.

WAR DIARY
or
INTELLIGENCE SUMMARY
(*Erase heading not required.*)

Place	Date	Hour	Summary of Events and Information	Remarks and references to Appendices
		3	A concentrated bombardment on WYTSCHAETE was carried out by heavy Howitzers of all calibres. It's hostily as co-operated with gas shell. During the afternoon a machine range was fired. A party of Infantry followed up the barrage and attacked the enemy's trenches near PECKHAM, returning with 16 prisoners. None was wounded. After patrolling activity and the ward of the enemy appears to be fresh. We lost 2 men killed and 3 wounded.	
		4	After today's trench range, the enemy's trenches were again attacked south of SPAN BROEK MOLEN. One officer and 21 O.R. were captured. Own losses were slight.	
		5	The usual trench range was carried out. Own artillery activity is increasing. The ammunition expenditure by the group for the 24 hours ending 5 p.m. was 2233 A, 1507 AX and 1647 BX. This represents about the daily average since the beginning of the month. In the early morning a hostile plane bombed an ammunition railhead near BAILLEUL destroying a quantity of ammunition.	

Army Form C. 2118.

WAR DIARY
or
INTELLIGENCE SUMMARY

(Erase heading not required.)

Place	Date	Hour	Summary of Events and Information	Remarks and references to Appendices
N26C96	June 1917 6		During the day final preparations were made and in the afternoon Col. Simpson moved to Battle Head Quarters with the 107th Infantry Brigade at Report Street Dugouts, N29 C 4.5. He took with him 2/Lt R.R. SHARP as Group Intelligence Officer, 2/Lt. V.C. MACORMINDALE also as Intelligence Officer, 2/Lt. E.F. ORR & E.G. STUDD as Group F.O.O.s and 2/Lt H.M. ACHILLES as Sgnal Officer. The Adjutant remained at N26 C 9.6. to supervise the ammunition supply.	
REGENT ST. DUGOUTS	7	3.10 a.m.	At 3.10 a.m. mines were exploded on the Corps front at PECKHAM, SPANBROEKMOLEN and KRUISSTRAAT and the attack was launched. There was no preliminary bombardment and only ordinary night firing preceded the attack. Every item of the enemy resistance was overcome and the entire programme was carried out without a hitch. The enemy did not put down an artillery Barrage. During the early morning a few Battery Sentries were engaged with H.V. Guns and some shells fired at our Balloons which all moved up during the night. No enemy active air service was prevalent from its appearing by our planes who engaged the enemy planes in the left keen aerodrome.	

WAR DIARY or INTELLIGENCE SUMMARY

Army Form C. 2118.

Place	Date	Hour	Summary of Events and Information	Remarks and references to Appendices
REGENT ST DUGOUTS	June 7		Between 8 and 8.30 a.m. the Batteries of the 173rd Brigade moved forward to positions near our old front line which had been previously prepared and stocked with 300 rounds per gun. By this time the Infantry was holding a line running roughly from the STEENYZER CABARET to LUMM FARM. Our line was held by the 107th & 109th Infantry Brigades. At about 3 p.m. the 11th Division reinforced by the 108th Brigade of the 36th Div. made a further attack on the OOSTTAVERNE LINE which they captured and held roughly from the WAMBEKE to POLKA ESTAMINET. It appears from prisoners' statements, that the second attack synchronised with the enemy's attempt to regain its ridge. No enemy made no serious counter attack. No casualties during the day were 2 Officers & 7 O.R. wounded. Both the Officers remained at duty. The total Casualties of the Division are reported to be under 1000. All the Guns & howitzers of the Brigade were actually in action at Zero hours. Between Zero about 12 midnight.	

Army Form C. 2118.

WAR DIARY
or
INTELLIGENCE SUMMARY
(Erase heading not required.)

Instructions regarding War Diaries and Intelligence Summaries are contained in F. S. Regs., Part II. and the Staff Manual respectively. Title Pages will be prepared in manuscript.

Place	Date	Hour	Summary of Events and Information	Remarks and references to Appendices
REGENT ST DUGOUTS	June 7		a period of over 20 hours only 7 18 pdrs went out of action. The chief causes were buffer trouble and jammed breech mechanisms. The average number of rounds fired per gun during the same period was 734, and the largest number fired by any one gun 1014.	
		8-16	During this period the line was taken over entirely by the Infantry of the 11th Division the 36th Division retiring to rest with the exception of the Divisional Artillery. The 173rd Brigade R.F.A. became attached to the Divisional Artillery. The 173rd Brigade RFA forming with the Right Sect. 59th Trench Mortar Bde RFA under the command of Lt. Col THOMSON 11th Division keft up a desultory fire on both slopes of the ridge. Belt occasional bursts of rapid firing on hostile positions of our front line. Enemy 15 H.V. Guns were active, His aircraft have become bolder and cage frequently often our lines occasionally exchange our Artillery machines. The sold on came for however, and their object often as a	

Army Form C. 2118.

WAR DIARY
or
INTELLIGENCE SUMMARY
(Erase heading not required.)

Instructions regarding War Diaries and Intelligence Summaries are contained in F. S. Regs., Part II. and the Staff Manual respectively. Title Pages will be prepared in manuscript.

Place	Date	Hour	Summary of Events and Information	Remarks and references to Appendices
REGENT ST. DUGOUTS	June 8-16		to be trusted to confidence of their Infantry. He is now making no attempt to hold a continuous line of trenches normally. Though from offering a good target to our Artillery. During the night there is considerable activity of patrols on both sides.	

	17		Major G.R.O. EDWARDS D.S.O. R.F.A. died of wounds received at 9 a.m. Lieut E.G. STUDD R.F.A. of the same Battery was wounded about same time. Lieut Col H.C. SIMPSON D.S.O. R.F.A. proceeded on leave to England. During his absence Major A.H. BURNE D.S.O. R.F.A. commands the Brigade. Batteries are now commanded as follows:
			A Battery Major W. ARNOLD
			B " " A.H. BURNE D.S.O.
			        (vacant)
			C " " C.L. CHAPMAN M.C.
			D " Capt. A.J. RUDDY
			     " " G.W. LEE
			     " " G.A. RICKARDS
			     " " W.A. EDMENSON	

2449 Wt. W14957/Mgo 750,000 1/16 J.B.C & A. Forms/C.2118/12.

WAR DIARY
or
INTELLIGENCE SUMMARY

Army Form C. 2118.

Place	Date	Hour	Summary of Events and Information	Remarks and references to Appendices
REGENT ST DUGOUTS	June 18th, 19th, 20th		Nothing of importance occurred. The Brigade marched out of the line to rest in the ST JANS CAPPEL Area. The Battery positions vacated here were taken over by another unit	
ST JANS CAPPEL	21st-25th		The Brigade remained at rest in the ST JANS CAPPEL Area. The period was occupied in overhauling equipment etc and in carrying out tactical schemes under Battery arrangements	
	26		The Brigade moved to their forward wagon lines, the Batteries re-occupying their old Battery positions during the night. The roads forward of SPANDBROEKMOLEN were subjected to intermittent shelling by the enemy, and D Battery had one horse killed. Several wounded	
REGENT ST	27		The Brigade relieved the 59th Brigade. There was considerable enemy artillery activity during the night. D Battery lost 6 O.R. wounded. Our Batteries engaged selected targets during the night. About 1500 x 18pdr & 250 4.5" how being fired	
DUGOUTS	28-29		Considerable enemy artillery activity	

Army Form C. 2118.

WAR DIARY
or
INTELLIGENCE SUMMARY

(*Erase heading not required.*)

Instructions regarding War Diaries and Intelligence Summaries are contained in F. S. Regs., Part II. and the Staff Manual respectively. Title Pages will be prepared in manuscript.

Place	Date	Hour	Summary of Events and Information	Remarks and references to Appendices
REGENTS DUGOUTS	June 29th		Lt. Col. H.E. Denham D.S.O. returned from leave and took over command of the Brigade.	
	30th		Nothing unusual happened.	

30.6.17

J.E.Peet
Lt. Col. R.F.A.
Commdg. 173 Bde. R.F.A.

Thy — Sep 1917
Missing

Army Form C. 2118.

173 Brigade R.F.A.
36th Div. IV Corps
Third Army

WAR DIARY or INTELLIGENCE SUMMARY

(Erase heading not required.)

Place	Date	Hour	Summary of Events and Information	Remarks and references to Appendices
P4c.85.80.	Oct 10-15 1917		A Redistribution of the guns of the Brigade took place & the following positions were occupied.	Ref Map 1/20000 Sheet 57C
			B/173. J.28.d.80.50 3 guns	
			J.35.b.8.5. 2 guns	
			C/173 J.36.a.08.85 3 guns	
			J.35.b.9.1. 2 guns	
			J.36.b.15-45 1 gun.	
			D/173 remained at J.35.a.5.2. & A/173 at Q.1.a.3.2.	
			At the same time A/173 again came under tactical command of the Brigade & the front to be covered was that of 39th Inf Bde and the Left Battalion of the 108th Inf Bde.	
	Oct 20-25		A/173 moved from Q.1.a.1 to a new position at P.5.a.0.8 (4 guns) with a lone gun at J.36.d.1.9. Two Howitzers of D/173 moved to J.36.a.67.	
			The policy of harassing fire by night continued during the preceding month & was continued & carried out so far as possible by the lone guns, which were only manned during the night.	

Army Form C. 2118.

WAR DIARY
or
INTELLIGENCE SUMMARY
(Erase heading not required.)

Instructions regarding War Diaries and Intelligence Summaries are contained in F. S. Regs., Part II. and the Staff Manual respectively. Title Pages will be prepared in manuscript.

Place	Date	Hour	Summary of Events and Information	Remarks and references to Appendices
			Hostile Artillery activity has been very slight. Retn of Counter Battery work attempted by the enemy was against the sector R.8/H.3 at R.13 & that 200 rounds were fired but the shooting was inaccurate & no damage was caused to personnel or equipment. Few Heavy & Medium Trench Mortars carried out organised bombardment & wire-cutting, supported by 18Pr enemy fire. One raid with artillery cooperation was attempted but not carried out owing to the Raiding Party being 3 sources & fired on by the enemy on their way over. No casualties. Gas Projectors were successfully fired on one occasion & Thermit shells were experimented with by 13/173 but without any visible results. A great deal of work was done on Battery positions, particularly by A & C Batteries who moved to new positions which had not previously been occupied. Gun pits were new & not weatherproof.	

Army Form C. 2118.

WAR DIARY
or
INTELLIGENCE SUMMARY
(Erase heading not required.)

Instructions regarding War Diaries and Intelligence Summaries are contained in F. S. Regs., Part II. and the Staff Manual respectively. Title Pages will be prepared in manuscript.

Place	Date	Hour	Summary of Events and Information	Remarks and references to Appendices
			and shaped hut[?] & all existing dugouts improved. Work on the second line started at B.v.5. Strong fatigues & an escort of the bad weather during the middle of the month. They were overtired on Oct 20th. Very many horses in horrible mud up to them. The weeks rest & a small party of men to rations were continued. Several football matches were arranged between batteries & also between battalions & infantry. The Divisional Bank visited the major times one evening & having contests on a small scale were started. The weather throughout the month has been wet.	

J.E.P.P[?]
Lieut R.F.A.
Commanding No. 80 R.F.A[?]

1/ 173 Bde. R.F.A. 36th Div.
WAR DIARY
IV Corps   Third Army

Nov. 1917   MAP
Date   Place   FRANCE Sheet
                                           57c N.E. 1/20,000
1-2   P4a 8.8   At the close of last month orders were received that prepar-
                  ations were to be made for an Offensive by the IV Corps.
                  Forward Battery Positions to the East of HERMIES were recon-
                  oitred and work on them started. Waking parties were
                  attached from the Horse Artillery. At this period Batteries
                  were located etc. as follows:—

                  Battery   Location   Commanded by   Second in
                                                                             Command

                  A/173   J 34 d 7.0   Major W. ARNOLD   Capt. F.J.H. HUNT
                  B/173 (3 guns)   J 28 d 8.8   }   "   A.H BURNE DSO. Capt. A.G PARSONS
                    "   "   J 33 b 8.5   }
                  C/173   J 36 a 08.85 }   Major R.L. THOMPSON MC. Capt. A.W JULIAN
                    "   (2 guns)   J 35 b 9.1 }
                  D/173   J 35 a 5.2   Major G.A. RICKARDS Capt. G.W LEE

WAR DIARY

Nov. 1917

DATE	PLACE	
1-2	Pt a 8.8	A and C Batteries also had Lone Guns in forward positions for Night firing. No definite orders for the offensive had been received at this period other than that Siegfried would be the chief feature of the attack. Consequently every effort was made to evidence to enemy to believe that there was no deflection from normal Trench Warfare. Harassing fire on a small scale was kept up during the night and occasional during the day. The enemy's artillery remained for the most part inactive.
3	BERTINCOURT	Brigade H.Q. moved to BERTINCOURT. Consequent on the above the 109th Infantry Brigade. During the night a raid was carried out by the 9th Royal Irish Fusiliers. 108th Infantry Brigade. Artillery Support was arranged by the 173rd Bde. and took the form of a Box Barrage round the objective of the raid in K 26 b. The raiders left our lines from YORKSHIRE BANK and proceeded N handled to the Canal on the Railside of it passing through the [crossed out] in the enemy wire at about K 26 d 3.9. [crossed out] Syrd from fire was opened by the Artillery on receipt of a light Signal from the Raiders. The raid was very successful though the enemy it is said to have resisted so strongly that it was not possible to bring in any prisoners. Enemy killed were estimated at 6 to 8 in our own

3.

WAR DIARY

Date	Place	
Nov. 1917		
3	BERTINCOURT	
4-18		

Casualties were light. The enemy put down a heavy barrage and howitzer [heavy] being rifle fire to bear on the party from pits to the North of WIGAN COPSE.

Preparations for the offensive were continued. With the exception of C/173, prepared a portion to the rear of HERMIES. These positions were just shelled from direct observation by the enemy at portions into either flash cover. Ammunition was laid down & weather-proof munitions, very little being made beyond platforms, and BC's hut. In some cases were ammunition dumps and a BC's hut. In some cases were was made of existing dugouts near the positions. These positions were located as follows: A/173 T 30 b 80.25; B/173 T 30 b 7.5; D/173 T 24 d 8.1. C/173 to accommodate 6 guns. During this T 36 a 08.25 so as to complete and 18 yd portion up during the light, so as to complete and 4·5 howitzers to 450 rounds per gun. Both B/173 and D/173 also howitzers stocked a proportion of Smoke Shell. D/173 also had a proportion of 106 fuze. The ammunition except in the case of C/173, was brought up by rail to T 29 b 3.0 and then a from there by pack. Ammunition for C/173 was unloaded at

WAR DIARY

Nov. 1917
Date / Place
18 BERTINCOURT

T 3 d 80.85 and later 15th position by vapor. On infestations were rendered less unwell were easy by its weather, which was exceptional by het with low visibility. little gun work was slow by even by aircraft. Each one less its later between to Screen light from dark and 16 present the effects of monsoonous fire in its neighbour-hood of tanks and buses.

Light ray by hay was continued and the usual procedure of Final Warfare was not departed from in particular except that use-acting at K20 c5.9 was carried out by Q/173. De wire was too thick to be effectually dealt with by 18 lbrs. Belts results were 'uneven' stained with 2"6" Trench Mortars using instantaneous fuze. G. the 14th Major A.H. Burne D.S.O. left to command "Q" Battery R.H.A. Command of B/173 was taken over by Capt A.G. PARSONS. On its light of the 18th 2 Sections per Battery moved into position. Lines of fire were carefully laid at it No Battery was allowed to open fire from its forward position before Zero. The remaining section of each Battery moved into position. Brigade let here not connected up. Telephone lines were laid in readiness before Zero. and no Shooting was allowed.

H.Q moved to K 25 a 3.0 Lieut Col M.C SIMPSON D.S.O. moved 15 the 109th Infantry Brigade H.Q. at K 7 d 2.0

19th "

15

WAR DIARY

Date	Place	
Nov.1917		
20th	K25a3.0	During the night 19/20th the enemy showed increased artillery activity. This was mainly directed on the horse of Kaffak or the roads, which was very loud before midnight. Gas was directed spasmodically at numerous points in the forward area, mostly from 10.5 cm howitzers, but it was desultory and unsustained. A Sm. of A Battery was put out of action and 3 men of B Battery wounded but little inconvenience was caused as our field artillery dispositions were complete early in the night before the shelling started. At zero hour, which was 6.20 a.m. covering the 109th Infantry Brigade was arranged as follows: A/173, C/173 & D/173 under the direct orders of the Group Commander at K7d 2.0 with 109 K 9.— Banky Brigade HQ. B/173 came under the orders of O.C 153rd Bde. 108th Infantry Bde. At Zero plus 175 minutes RFA covering the 108th Infantry Brigade was loaned, the Cdr. of the 173rd and 280th Bdes. RFA came under the orders of Lieut-Col. H.C Sempton. D.S.O. This artillery was divided into 2 sub-groups the 280th Bde. RFA. with H.Q at DENICOURT and the 173rd Bde. RFA. with H.Q at K25a3.0. C/173 moved forward to a new position at K26a 7.0. The attack of the 109th Infantry Bde. was directed at the SPOIL HEAP in K20. When this was seized the attack moved 15th North and cleared up all Trenches 15th West of the Canal as far North as the 2nd line running E+W between E26 a + b and E26 c+D while they joined up with the 169th Infantry Bde. on the

Army Form C. 2118.

WAR DIARY
or
INTELLIGENCE SUMMARY.
(Erase heading not required)

Instructions regarding War Diaries and Intelligence Summaries are contained in F. S. Regs., Part II. and the Staff Manual respectively. Title pages will be prepared in manuscript.

Place	Date Nov. 1917	Hour	Summary of Events and Information	Remarks and references to Appendices
DEMICOURT	26		The Artillery covering the Divisional Front was reinforced during the night. The 6th Heavy Regt. (2nd Div.) relieved its equivalent, and the 2nd Div. Artillery came into the line.	App. 1
	27		The Artillery was again to be reinforced. Nothing unusual occurred.	App. 2
	28		A further reinforcement of the Artillery took place.	App. 3
	29			
	30		At 7.30 a.m. the enemy heavily attacked on the whole front with large forces supported by a very strong artillery. Our batteries in their English sights and places as far as YTRES and VELU were fired a lot. H.V. guns on DEMICOURT in particular, heavy shelling and a shrapnel 10 a.m. a few gas shell were fired into the village which caused considerable casualties. The attack lasted until about 15 hours later. Hb found on its front, the 6 it enemy attack made on the lines of the Infantry Regts. and armoured cars which caused to the enemy. The batteries were drawn forward and coming into action and took shelter of the 173 at Ruyals the wounded 18 had moved	

(A7092). Wt. W12839/M.293. 75,000. 1/17. D. D. & L., Ltd. Forms/C.2118.14.

Army Form C. 2118.

WAR DIARY
or
INTELLIGENCE SUMMARY.
(Erase heading not required.)

Instructions regarding War Diaries and Intelligence Summaries are contained in F. S. Regs., Part II. and the Staff Manual respectively. Title pages will be prepared in manuscript.

Place	Date	Hour	Summary of Events and Information	Remarks and references to Appendices
R25a3.0	Nov. 1917 20		Relieved the 108th Infant Brigade on the Right. About 8 from 21-73 Relief commenced shortly before zero hour. The O.C. reported when 3 men of B Battn were wounded and a few of A Battn. During the movement the Brigade moved forward to position in the neighbourhood of K9 central. There was a good deal of rain and the roads were in a very bad state of Bn.	
DEMICOURT	21		At 6 pm the 109th Infant Brigade was relieved by the 108th Bde. Lt Col Simpson remained at Infantry Bde H.Q. at K7 d 2.0. The remainder of the H.Q. went at DEMICOURT.	
	22		MOEUVRES was attacked and overlooked but was retaken. On the evening later on the day. By this time the the enemy had offered considerable and it began to be attacked. Itd Bn Bn had though up to stop reinforcements about the time the enemy began to develop more attacks.	
	23			
	24 25		10 am Batteries The 109th Bde, relieved the 108th Bde. Military mutual arrived	

WAR DIARY
or
INTELLIGENCE SUMMARY

Army Form C. 2118.

Place	Date	Hour	Summary of Events and Information	Remarks and references to Appendices
Trenches	Nov 20		[Text largely illegible due to faded handwriting] Fired by the East of [...] the City. Was the object and an Object of [...] fire. By nightfall the situation had been almost entirely [...] as [...] restored. No [...] Our [...] 8" [...] Gun Battery Observation was on [...] given to the infantry to the subjects of our own [...] Our Casualties [...] in excess [...] Commanding the 8" [...] We are at the front of the 8th [...] and were slightly reduced as an infantry engagement and were [...] dealt with by the [...] [...] to our own attendance on [...] Officers were [...] [...] in the day Capt A E Parsons was wounded. No Signallers [...] 19 other [...] personnel during the day. [...] [...] approximately 19,000 rounds 7am to 7pm. No. [...] [...] [...] [...] B Battery fired 3,800 and [...] 6 [...] [...] [...] thrilled.	

H.C. Pirt
Lieut Col R.F.A.
Commanding 178 Bde. R.F.A.

WAR DIARY
or
INTELLIGENCE SUMMARY.
(Erase heading not required.)

Army Form C. 2118.

173 Brigade R.F.A.
36th Division

Vol 27 226

Place	Date	Hour	Summary of Events and Information	Remarks and references to Appendices
DEMICOURT	December 1917		At this time the Brigade functioned as a Sub-Group under the direct orders of Lieut Col H.C. SIMPSON D.S.O. who commanded the Main Group R.F.A. covering the 6th Infantry Brigade of the 2nd Division. Brigade H.Q. were at DEMICOURT but the Batteries of the Brigade received orders direct from the Main Group Commander, who was at Infantry Brigade H.Q. at K7d 9.0. At a time when the enemy was making repeated heavy counter attacks and the Artillery were continually being called upon to carry out unexpected tasks at short notice the Main Group system of Artillery Organisation was once again tested and found to work admirably. Batteries were all in the immediate vicinity of the Main Group Commander and communications worked very satisfactorily. The closest possible liaison existed between Infantry, Artillery, and the Machine Gun Corps, information from all sources being passed on automatically as soon as received, and the want through co-ordination of effort being achieved. During the early morning 8 men of Brigade H.Q. returned at DEMICOURT	Ref Map FRANCE Sheet 57c N.W. 1:20,000

WAR DIARY or INTELLIGENCE SUMMARY

Army Form C. 2118.

Place	Date	Hour	Summary of Events and Information	Remarks and references to Appendices
DEMICOURT	December 1917			
	1		became casualties owing to enemy gas shells fired during the previous day. 10 other officers and men were also affected but were able to remain at duty. After the enemy's first effort of the previous day further counter attacks were constantly expected but did not develop during the day. Battery Commanders went in person to the O.P. and a careful look out was kept. The situation was declared considerably more easy to deal with owing to the fact that an excellent view of the Bois Couloi be obtained from Hants Trench H.Q. During the day Major R.L. THOMPSON M.C. who commanded C Battery was killed while creeping out observation out. Thanks the noble attitude & bearing of the Essex Regt who had been cut-off and surrounded at Lock 5 but without success this last leave of this batty had been determined to fight to the end.	
	3		Orders were received that it had been decided to shorten the later	

WAR DIARY
or
INTELLIGENCE SUMMARY.
(Erase heading not required.)

Army Form C. 2118.

Place	Date	Hour	Summary of Events and Information	Remarks and references to Appendices
	December 1917			
DEMICOURT	3	3 b	Front and 11th Batteries would be withdrawn during the night to positions near HERMIES. Orders were issued to Battery Commanders in person. The greatest hostile security lamp ordered and the move was completed without molestation. One gun per Battery was left in the old position and just before dawn with sufficient ammunition to keep up a slow fire all night, the remainder of guns moving immediately to after dark. The move was completed without casualties and all stores and ammunition were removed. Brigade H.Q. moved to BEAUMETZ, the front observation being taken up and Battery Wagon Lines [unclear] to the way bow head of VELU WOOD. The Brigade came under the orders of the 56th Division forming with the 280 Bde RFA a forces under the Command	
BEAUMETZ		4.5	The situation remained the quick battle artillery action front with no change of any kind except fire directed against back areas.	Lt Col SOUTHAM.
T 12 b		6	The Brigade relieved the Batteries of the 5th Horse Artillery Brigade in the neighbourhood of DOIGNIES. Bde H.Q. being at T 12 b. The Brigade passed a Sub fort with Lt Col SHORT-STEWART DSO	

WAR DIARY
or
INTELLIGENCE SUMMARY.
(Erase heading not required.)

Army Form C. 2118.

Place	Date	Hour	Summary of Events and Information	Remarks and references to Appendices
I 12 b	December 1917			
	6		as Main Body Commander, the Group being under the orders of the 51st (Highland) Division.	
		6-12	At this time Intelligence was received that the Enemy was contemplating an attack with Tanks captured from us supplemented possibly by others of his own manufacture. All precautions were accordingly taken. O.P.s with suitable fields of view were selected, positions for single guns to deal with individual Tanks were reconnoitred and Special Barrages on likely points of attack were arranged. Also all Battery positions were wired in so as to be suitable strong points should our front system be pierced. Favoured by the clear frosty weather the Enemy showed great Aerial activity during this period and the bombing of back areas on a large scale was carried out. During the day Enemy Aircraft showed fact, daring in their reconnaissance flights, flying low over Battery positions. To deal with these A.A. Lewis Guns per Brigade were issued at	

WAR DIARY
or
INTELLIGENCE SUMMARY.

Army Form C. 2118.

Place	Date	Hour	Summary of Events and Information	Remarks and references to Appendices
I 12 b	December 1917	6-12	Were located at Battery Centres and manned by detachments of Infantry. The intention being that Artillery personnel should subsequently be trained in the use of this weapon. As a defence against bombing attacks orders were issued that all huts and Billets at Battery Wagon Lines should be surrounded by earth walls. On several occasions bombs were dropped in the neighbourhood of Wagon lines, but no casualties to men or animals occurred. During this period the situation remained quiet.	
HAVRINCOURT WOOD	12		The Brigade was transferred to the METZ front, relieving the 310th Bde R.F.A. and coming under the orders of the 20th Div. Artillery who were attached to the 47th Division. Batteries took up positions to the East of HAVRINCOURT WOOD, Wagon lines being near SOREL-LE GRAND.	
	13		The weather continued cold and frosty, but with low visibility. The ground was probably covered with snow. Nothing of importance occurred.	
BEAUCAMP	14		The Brigade moved to the neighbourhood of BEAUCAMP, relieving	

Army Form C. 2118.

WAR DIARY
or
INTELLIGENCE SUMMARY.
(Erase heading not required.)

Place	Date	Hour	Summary of Events and Information	Remarks and references to Appendices
BEAUCAMP	December 1917	14	The 306th Bde. R.F.A. and comp under the orders of the 30th Div. Artillery.	
	14-18	During this period prisoners of [Lessay?] line was carried out by light and day. The enemy showed no unusual activity. Counter attack was never considered to be a menace but its utmost vigilance was maintained. The hostile entrenched lines suffered heavily there and the personnel of Batteries and wagon suffered from the cold. Although Battle Casualties were extremely low, a large number of men were evacuated with sick.	
	19	The Batteries of the Brigade passed under the orders of Lieut-Col. H.C. SIMPSON D.S.O. assuming M.C. POTTER D.S.O. Right Half. War Group consisting of the 306th Bde. R.F.A. and the 119th Bde. R.F.A.	
	20	Nothing unusual occurred.	
	21	C and D Batteries 306th Bde. were withdrawn in the Right Group by C & D Batteries 173 W Bde. being replaced.	
	22	From 3.30 a.m. until dawn the enemy carried out a very heavy bombardment on the Sector pass of the left front. Gas shell	

Army Form C. 2118.

WAR DIARY
or
INTELLIGENCE SUMMARY.
(Erase heading not required.)

Instructions regarding War Diaries and Intelligence Summaries are contained in F.S. Regs., Part II. and the Staff Manual respectively. Title pages will be prepared in manuscript.

Place	Date	Hour	Summary of Events and Information	Remarks and references to Appendices
BEAUCAMP	December 1917 22		was liberally used, and an attempt was made to localise an Battalion. However no Infantry attack developed. The Artillery was under Lieut Col H.C. SIMPSON D.S.O. assuming command of the Centre Group, consisting of No 179th Bde R.F.A., 232 Brigade R.F.A., D Battery of the 298th Brigade R.F.A. and C + D Batteries of the 173rd Brigade R.F.A.	
	23-25		Nothing of importance occurred. The policy of harassing fire day and night was continued. The hostile Batteries in the neighbourhood of BOAR COPSE were heavily shelled on several occasions by the enemy, but without appreciable result.	
BEAULEN- COURT	26		The Brigade was relieved by the 223rd Brigade R.F.A and proceeded to the BEAULENCOURT Staying Area. The march was carried out with real difficulty as a heavy frost set in & snow began to fall rendered the roads extremely slippery.	
	27-31		As the roads were impassable for horsed transport owing to the continuation of the severe weather the Brigade was unable to resume its march out of the Area.	

H.C.B
Lieut Col R.F.A.
Commanding 173 Bde. R.F.A.

173rd Brigade, R.F.A.
36th Division,
VIII Corps,
5th Army

Army Form C. 2118.

WAR DIARY
or
INTELLIGENCE SUMMARY.
(Erase heading not required.)

Instructions regarding War Diaries and Intelligence Summaries are contained in F.S. Regs, Part II. and the Staff Manual respectively. Title pages will be prepared in manuscript.

Place	Date	Hour	Summary of Events and Information	Remarks and references to Appendices
BUIRE	Jan. 1.1918	9am	The Brigade left the BEAUVANCOURT area on the morning of 1st. proceeded to BUIRE, where it billeted for night 1/2nd. The march was continued on the morning of 2nd Jan. when the Brigade proceeded to, and arrived in the Corbie area (HAMEL) during the afternoon of 2nd.	Appx. I.
HAMEL	2/7		Brigade billetted in HAMEL from Jan. 2. to 7th.	
LE QUESNEL	7/11		Brigade proceeded to LE QUESNEL on 7th Jan. and arrived during afternoon of that day. Remained in Billets in LE QUESNEL until 11th.	
ROISGLISE	11/13		Proceeded from LE QUESNEL to ROYE area (ROISGLISE) and remained in Billets until 13th.	Appx. 2.
HAPPENCOURT	13		In accordance with instructions the Brigade marched from ROISGLISE on 13th and arrived at HAPPENCOURT during the afternoon of that day. Arrangements were at once proceeded with in connection with relieving the 56th French Divisional Artillery and on the evening of the 13th, B.C. and D. Batteries sent one gun into the line.	
	14th		On the morning of 14th the Brigade Commander reported and reporting Officers proceeded to H.Q. located at A.31.d. O.8. in order to properly relieve the 56th French Division Artillery.	

T.2134. Wt. W708-776. 500000. 4/15. Sir J. C. & S.

WAR DIARY
or
INTELLIGENCE SUMMARY.
(Erase heading not required.)

Army Form C. 2118.

Instructions regarding War Diaries and Intelligence Summaries are contained in F. S. Regs., Part II. and the Staff Manual respectively. Title pages will be prepared in manuscript.

Place	Date	Hour	Summary of Events and Information	Remarks and references to Appendices
	Jan 1916 14th cont.		commence the duties of taking over Batteries B.C.D. sent two more guns into action on night 14th/15th.	
		15th	Batteries and the remainder of their guns into the line on night 15/16th Jan' and the following were the locations & units of the Brigade on the morning of the 16th Jan'	

Unit.	Position.	no. of guns.	Commanders.
H.Q. 173.	A.30.d.0.8.		Major R.C. Empson. R.F.A.
A.173.	G.5.d.5.H	2	Capt. S.R. Abbott. R.F.A.
B.173.	A.30.d.9.9.	4	" H.R.G. Gunner. R.F.A.
	B.25.a.1.8.	2	
C.173.	B.25.b.5.8.	4	" R.N. Dicey. R.F.A.
	B.19.d.4.5.	2	
D.173.	A.24.b.0.1.	4	Major G.A. Ricketts M.G. R.F.A.
	B.19.c.2.6.	2	

| | | 16th | The Brigade Commander finally took over from the French on the morning of 16th and arrangements for the defence of the line were | |

WAR DIARY
or
INTELLIGENCE SUMMARY.

(Erase heading not required.)

Army Form C. 2118.

Instructions regarding War Diaries and Intelligence Summaries are contained in F. S. Regs., Part II. and the Staff Manual respectively. Title pages will be prepared in manuscript.

Place	Date	Hour	Summary of Events and Information	Remarks and references to Appendices
	Apr 1918. 16th Cont.		further about, the Brigade covered the 109th Inty. Brigade holding a line from B.10.d.6.7 to B.8a.1.6 and S.O.S. lines were allotted to batteries of this Brigade as under:—	
			A/173. B.8c.7.0 - B.10.d.6.7. inclusive.	
			B/173. B.8.d.7.0 - B.9d.6.8.	
			C/173. B.9.d.6.8 - B.10.d.6.7.	
			D/173. B.9.a.2.1 - B.8.2.2.	
			Two 18 pdrs Batteries were attached to the Brigade, making a total of six Batteries which comprised the Right group, which was commanded by Major R.C. EMPSON R.F.A. Batteries, Position, "vacations", S.O.S. lines were as follows, Commanding officer.	
			Unit. Position. no. of guns. S.O.S. lines. Commanding officer.	
			A/14.A.F.Bde. G.5.a.1.2. 4. B.8a.1.5 - B.8.d.7.0. Major W.S.Wigata Gray. M.C R.F.A	
			G.4.d.J.6. 2. B.8a.1.5 - B.8.d.7.0.	
			88 Bty. A.23.b.5.4. 4. Capt. C.M.Dunham. R.F.A.	
			A.29.b.0.2. 2.	

Army Form C. 2118.

WAR DIARY
or
INTELLIGENCE SUMMARY.
(Erase heading not required.)

Instructions regarding War Diaries and Intelligence Summaries are contained in F. S. Regs., Part II. and the Staff Manual respectively. Title pages will be prepared in manuscript.

Place	Date	Hour	Summary of Events and Information	Remarks and references to Appendices
	Jan. 1918.			
	17/19		Batteries have been doing as little shooting as possible in order that both occupied and unoccupied positions could be given as much attention as possible, no positions taken over by this Brigade requires a considerable amount of work on them to bring them up to our requirements.	
			The situation during this period has been very quiet, most work on positions has been going ahead, and already there is an appreciable difference in the appearance of Battery positions at the front.	
			On 17th Jan. the 147th Army lines of this Brigade moved from HAPPENCOURT to TUGNY-ET-PONT.	App. J.
	19/21		Quiet.	
	22.		At 9 p.m. an order was received from H.Q. 2nd Army to open fire on S.O.S. lines owing to a German raid on our left. This was opened with apparently successful results as nothing further was heard. Information was received later that out Infantry lost 1 other rank.	

T2134. Wt. W708-776. 500000. 4/15. Sir J. C. & S.

Army Form C. 2118.

WAR DIARY
or
INTELLIGENCE SUMMARY.
(Erase heading not required.)

Instructions regarding War Diaries and Intelligence Summaries are contained in F. S. Regs., Part II. and the Staff Manual respectively. Title pages will be prepared in manuscript.

Place	Date	Hour	Summary of Events and Information	Remarks and references to Appendices
	Jan 1918			
	22nd cont.		taken prisoner were 1 other rank missing.	
	23rd to 26th		Quiet.	
	27th		Lt. Col. H.C. Denham, D.S.O. R.F.A. returned from leave and took over Command of RIGHT GROUP, 36th Divl. Arty.	
	28th		Quiet.	
	29th		Quiet. Enemy patrols active.	
	30th		"	
	31st		Situation quiet.	

H C D
Lt. Col. R.F.A.
Commanding 173rd Bde. R.F.A.

WAR DIARY or INTELLIGENCE SUMMARY

Army Form C. 2118.

173 Brigade R.F.A.
36th Div. XVIII Corps, Fifth Army

Place	Date	Hour	Summary of Events and Information	Remarks and references to Appendices
A30 b.08.	February 1918		At this period the Brigade, with A/114 and the 88th Battery formed the Right Group, 36th Divisional Artillery. During the whole month the attitude of the enemy was unimpressive, and the general situation was extremely quiet. The enemy contented himself with occasional shots on Bellicourt and O.P.'s, and shot less bombardment growth in the forward area with far less. No undue firing impressions were carried out by us other than the registration of new Anti-Aircraft Batteries during photographic flights and occasional counter-battery shots with 4.5 Howitzers. Orders were received that fewer of the enemy less than 20 should we not be fired on, an exception being made in the case of small parties of German officers seen up dressing our lines. Reconnaissances of the salient were very frequent. Enemy aircraft activity was very marked, on balloon's being attacked during the day on several occasions and bombing operations on a large scale being carried out at night. Enemy Anti-Aircraft batteries were extremely active and accurate, especially those in the neighbourhood of St-Quentin. In fact he seems anxious to prevent an observation of the town.	Ref. Map France Sheet 66C N.W. 1:20,000

WAR DIARY or INTELLIGENCE SUMMARY

Army Form C. 2118.

Place	Date	Hour	Summary of Events and Information	Remarks and references to Appendices
A.30 b.0.8	Feb. 19/18		In spite of the quiet attitude of the enemy, the intelligence that we received during the previous week that the enemy was contemplating an attack on the front was confirmed. The execution of this attack and reinforcing battery positions was carried a with the greatest speed, and no attempt on its side to rouse the enemy. Shells & other fire were proceeded with without interruption. The organisation of the Artillery in depth was carried out as laid down in B.H.Q. (Artillery) Notes. Every preparation was also made for the arrival of reinforcing Brigades, positions being prepared, and zones, O.P.'s allotted. The only casualties sustained by the Brigade during the week were 1 Officer and 3 Other Ranks wounded. The weather for the most part was dry with a good deal of haze about the middle of the month. Defence arrangements were amended and consolidated as shewn in the attached Order. A number of reinforcing Brigades for the Subject of Flank Protection both in the case of hostile attack and for purposes of Counter Preparation were instructed. Also lazed Barrages to be surfaces against Hostile lazed attacks.	App. 1

Army Form C. 2118.

WAR DIARY
or
INTELLIGENCE SUMMARY.
(Erase heading not required.)

Place	Date	Hour	Summary of Events and Information	Remarks and references to Appendices
GRAND SERAUCOURT	Jan. 1-13		Nothing unusual occurred. Brest H.Q moved on 12th to GRAND SERAUCOURT	
	14		C/193 stood by to operate in a raid to be carried out by the 151st R.I.R and left point. They were not called upon to fire	App. II
	15-16		The 88th Battery and A/112 were relieved by the 383rd Battery + the 462nd Battery, coming under the orders of O.C. Right Sect.	
AUG 2.8	21		Right H.Q moved to C/14 & 2.8. Defence arrangements were revised as shown in order attached.	App. III
	23			
	27		Information was received that a Captured Enemy Airman let the Enemy would probably attack on March 2nd and 3rd. In & arrangements for defence were accordingly made	
	28		Abnormal movement in the enemy lines near LA PRE ALLER and elsewhere was observed though the day including bodies of officers moving on line. Then with range these two fired on. The enemy's artillery remained unresponsive	

H.C.A.
Lieut Col R.F.A.
Commanding 193 Bgde R.F.A.

36th Divisional Artillery.

173rd BRIGADE R. F. A.

M A R C H   1 9 1 8

Appendices attached :)

        Account of operations 21st-31st

        Barrage tables.

        Artillery Instructions.

        Targets

WAR DIARY or INTELLIGENCE SUMMARY

Army Form C. 2118.

173rd Brigade R.F.A.
36th Division.
XVIII Corps. Fifth Army.

Place	Date	Hour	Summary of Events and Information	Remarks and references to Appendices
	March 1918		Reference maps: France 62.c. 1/40,000; St Quentin 1/100,000 and Amiens 1/200,000.	
G.14.b.2.8.1st.	1st		Final defensive arrangements were made in expectation of the enemy attack on March 2nd. Special barrages were ordered to be put down in the event of the enemy breaking on our front line of Resistance.	App. I.
	2nd		At 8.30 p.m. a heavy enemy trench mortar bombardment took place on the front of the group on our Right, and there was also some trench mortar activity on our own front. N.F. was called for by the Group on our Right, and given. It subsequently appeared that during the bombardment the enemy raided a post held by our Right Infantry Brigade and captured some prisoners. Some snow fell during the day. The situation remained abnormally quiet. Information was received that during the previous night the enemy carried out raids on a large scale along the whole length of the front front. Prisoners stated that a continuation of these efforts was to be expected on the British front, the object of the enemy being to test our strength at various points. Locuanany counter-measures were taken and the utmost vigilance was observed. It is considered that the information received from a captured enemy summer on 27th February referred to	

Army Form C. 2118.

WAR DIARY
or
INTELLIGENCE SUMMARY.
(Erase heading not required.)

Instructions regarding War Diaries and Intelligence Summaries are contained in F. S. Regs., Part II. and the Staff Manual respectively. Title pages will be prepared in manuscript.

Place	Date	Hour	Summary of Events and Information	Remarks and references to Appendices
	2nd.		these were entrenched and not to a general attack. The orders concerning Group Rocket Guards were revised and re-issued.	App. II.
	3rd.		A vigorous policy of harassing fire was ordered by the XVIII Corps. Fire programme were carried out at night in conjunction with the Heavy Artillery Group concentrations were formulated, and an aggressive an attitude as possible was adopted. As a rule, only Batteries in forward positions in front of the Battle Zone, were called upon to fire but in the case of Corps concentrations all guns and howitzers which could bear, took part. A list of Group concentrations is attached.	App. III.
	4th.		Throughout the day, enemy patrols showed most extraordinary activity along the whole front. Large parties approached our lines in the neighbourhood of SPHINX WOOD. (B.17.c.) and near PIRE ALLER. These were engaged by our Artillery with remarkable effect, and the Infantry captured a number of prisoners. These stated that the enemy was under the impression that we had evacuated our forward system and that their orders were to confirm this and, if possible, occupy our trenches in force.	

Army Form C. 2118.

WAR DIARY
or
INTELLIGENCE SUMMARY.
(Erase heading not required.)

Instructions regarding War Diaries and Intelligence Summaries are contained in F.S. Regs., Part II. and the Staff Manual respectively. Title pages will be prepared in manuscript.

Place	Date	Hour	Summary of Events and Information	Remarks and references to Appendices
	5th & 6th		Nothing unusual occurred.	
	7th		Group "S.O.S." lines were altered so as to bring the Barrage nearer to our Outpost line.	App. IV
	8th		The attack list of Targets was circulated. Special attention was paid to those in harassing fire.	App. V
	9th		The weather at this time was extraordinarily fine and warm. Ground visibility was exceptionally good.	
	10th		Nothing unusual occurred. The enemy Artillery remained inactive.	
	11th		Supplementary Barrages were ordered for use in case the enemy should be able to launch his attack before the normal S.O.S. Barrage could be brought down, and in case the line of Resistance should be broken. It was still expected that the enemy offensive would be in the nature of a surprise attack with the aid of a large number of Tanks. Prisoners on several occasions gave accurate descriptions of a new pattern German Tank which they said was being manufactured in large numbers. 2 Anti Tank Guns were placed in position ^ on the Group front. They were in charge	App. VI & VII

A 5834. Wt: W4973/M687. 750,000 8/16. D.D. & L. Ltd. Forms/C.2118/13.

Army Form C. 2118.

WAR DIARY
or
INTELLIGENCE SUMMARY.
(Erase heading not required.)

Instructions regarding War Diaries and Intelligence Summaries are contained in F. S. Regs., Part I. and the Staff Manual respectively. Title pages will be prepared in manuscript.

Place	Date	Hour	Summary of Events and Information	Remarks and references to Appendices
	12th		of an Officer. Arrangements were also made for dealing with any tanks which succeeded in breaking through the forward system. A special course of Training in Anti-Tank Defence was instituted at the Fifth Army Artillery School near R.D.V.E., selected detachments being sent for instruction. A special 18-pr. carriage allowing a traverse of 50° was improvised by the Royal Engineers. Throughout the period every effort was made to complete work on Battery positions and O.P.o. O.C. Right Group was given control of all work in the forward zone, orders being issued by him from time to time to all Batteries of the Divisional Artillery in the Line. A specimen order is attached. Arrangements were made for covering the line of Strong Points and the Battle Zone.	App. VII.
	13th		Further Lefft arrangements and Special Barrages to deal with Loose Attacks at different points were revised and re-issued.	App. VIII.
	14th		At this time attention was drawn to groups of apparently hostile objects which appeared behind the enemy lines, great numbers of these objects were located by the Air Service, mostly to the North of the River. The hypothesis that they were	App. X.

Army Form C. 2118.

WAR DIARY
or
INTELLIGENCE SUMMARY.

(Erase heading not required.)

Place	Date	Hour	Summary of Events and Information	Remarks and references to Appendices
	15th/16th		Tanks was abandoned, owing to their small size. It is believed that they were light tractors of a new pattern, designed for drawing Field Guns, and carrying Ammunition.	
	17th		Situation remained quiet, the aggressive attitude of our own Artillery provoking very little response from the enemy. Information was received that the enemy had carried out bombardments with Gas Shell to the west of CAMBRAI on a scale greater than anything hitherto experienced. It was feared that Bombardments of a similar nature might be carried out on our own front, where the terrain was particularly suitable. If this had been done, it would have involved the elimination of the 3 Batteries of the Group, which were in position in the Forward Zone. Arrangements were, therefore, immediately made to withdraw to Rear positions as many guns as could be spared. The very greatest Anti-Gas measures were also taken. All Batteries were provided with gloves for their detachments; dugouts, telephone pits, and Command Posts were rendered Gas-proof as far as possible, and quantities of Chloride of Lime issued to Batteries for the purpose of neutralizing gas-shell craters.	App. XI.

WAR DIARY or INTELLIGENCE SUMMARY

Army Form C. 2118.

Place	Date	Hour	Summary of Events and Information	Remarks and references to Appendices
	18th		At about this time Aeroplane photographs coupled with information obtained from deserters revealed the presence of large numbers of new tunnel emplacements in the enemy's lines. These were made to resemble shell-craters from which they were hardly distinguishable. The great number of these gave rise to the supposition that the enemy would rely on giving a feeling in our Forward Zone by these means rather than by the use of tanks. These emplacements, and the areas in which they were present in the largest numbers, were heavily dealt with by Artillery fire.	
	19th		Definite information was obtained from enemy deserters that the enemy attack would take place on the morning of the 21st. These deserters testified to the enormous concentration of troops behind the enemy's lines, large numbers of which had actually taken up their position in dugouts in the enemy front line. Harassing fire was therefore prosecuted more vigorously than ever. A specimen of the Barrage fired is attached.	
Q.8.A.1.2.	20th		Headquarters were moved to Q.8.A.1.2. All Artillery in the Forward Zone was withdrawn to Rear positions at 10.30 pm after carrying out a heavy bombardment programme which provoked no response from the enemy. Fire was maintained more or less continuously throughout the night	App. XII

WAR DIARY
or
INTELLIGENCE SUMMARY.

(Erase heading not required.)

Army Form C. 2118.

Place	Date	Hour	Summary of Events and Information	Remarks and references to Appendices
	21st		The enemy bombardment opened at 4.35 a.m. An account of the operations from the 21st to the 31st March 1918 is attached. During the latter period the Casualties of the Brigade were as follows. Killed :- 2/Lt E.F.B. ORR. R.F.A and 13 other Ranks. Wounded :- Lt (A/Major) G.A RICKARDS M.C R.F.A) and 38 other Ranks 2/Lt H.W. BODGER R.F.A) Missing Lt E.T. SCOTT. R.F.A. 2/Lt E.G. PARFITT and 37 other Ranks	App XIII.

G.W.R.
Major R.F.A
Commanding 173rd Brigade R.F.A.

SECRET   173rd Bde. No.S.3/21

O.C.
    A,B,C, and D/173
    A/153
    B, and D/153 (Detached Sections)
    462 Battery R.F.A.
    H.Q. 107 Infy. Bde.
    H.Q. 108 Infy. Bde.
    Left Group

The following barrages will be worked out and arrangements made to carry them out in case the enemy pierces our first line of resistance.

Barrage "X" For the defence of forward strong points
C/173	Barrage from	B.13.a.7.6.	to B.13.a.5.6.
A/173	" "	B.15.c.95.90.	to B.14.d.90.90.
B/173	" "	B.14.d.90.90.	to B.14.d.55.90.
462	" "	B.14.d.55.90.	to B.14.d.25.90.
D/173	" "	B.15.c.90.85.	to B.15.c.35.85.

Barrage "Y" For the defence of the strong point line by day
462	Barrage from	A.17.b.60.60.	to A.17.b.15.55.
D/153	2 guns fire on road		
A/173	3 guns barrage	A.18.a.90.90.	to A.18.c.70.85.
"	"	A.18.d.95.95.	to A.18.b.70.15.
D/173	Barrage	B.20.a.50.00.	to B.19.b.90.20.
A/153	2 guns barrage	B.19.b.80.30.	to B.19.b.60.25.
B/153	2 " "	B.19.b.60.20.	to B.19.b.40.15.

Barrage "Z" For the defence for the strong point line by night
462	Enfilade	A.11.d.20.15.	to A.17.b.30.50.
A/173	Barrage	B.19.a.45.45.	to B.19.a.10.30.
A/153	2 guns barrage	B.19.b.55.40.	to B.19.b.40.30.
B/153	2 " "	B.18.c.90.60.	to B.18.c.75.70.
D/153	2 " fire on road	A.18.a.90.10.	to A.18.c.70.85.

2.3.18.

                                Capt. R.F.A.
                         Adjt. 173rd Bde. R.F.A.

App II

SECRET

173rd Brigade R.F.A. No. S.3./116/7.

    O.C. A/173.
         B/173.
         C/173.
         D/173.
    462 Battery R.F.A.
(2) H.Q. 36th Divl. Artillery.
H.Q. 107th Inf. Brigade.
     108th Inf. Brigade
Left Group R.F.A.

The following is substituted for the instructions as to manning of Rocket Guards issued under my No. S.3./116/4. of 22.2.18.

Rocket Guards will be mounted as ordered in 36th Divisional Artillery Order No. 32 dated 20.2.18.

The Guard at JEANNET will be found permanently by C/173 Battery.

The Guard at ARLOIN will now be mounted at the newly established O.P. at B.19.a.65.70. and will be found permanently by A/173 Battery R.F.A.

The Rocket Guard at A.30.b.0.8 whose duty it is to report all signals on Right and Centre Brigade Fronts will be found by B/173 and D/173 alternately commencing with B/173 on 4.3.18.
The O's.C. B/173 and D/173 will arrange to mount the Guard and have it visited by an Officer during its tour of duty and they are responsible that the Guard knows its instructions.

The Guard at JEANNET will instantly report any S.O.S. signals sent up on the front held by 108th Infantry Brigade, likewise the Guard at B.19.a.65.70. will report signals sent up from 107th Infantry Brigade front and at the same time they will report to Group Headquarters by telephone giving the bearing of the Rocket from their O.P.

If a Rocket goes up on any front other than as above the bearing is to be at once reported to Group Headquarters by telephone.

In this case no repeating rockets are to be fired.
Rocket Guards are to be mounted at dusk and dismount one hour after dawn.

Captain R.F.A.
Adjutant 173rd Brigade R.F.A.

2. 3. 18.

173rd Brigade No. C.70.

O.C.   A/173
        B/173
        C/173   Reference 1/20,000 Map Sheet
        D/173   66 c. Edition 3.A.
        462 Battery R.F.A.
H.Q. 107th Infy Bde.)
       108th " ") For information

The following Concentrations are to be arranged. They will be ordered by their code name followed by the time of firing.
The rates of fire will be as fast as possible consistent with good laying.
A.X. will not be fired at ranges over 3600 yards unless fuzed with instantaneous fuze or if firing at dugouts.

CODE WORD		TASKS
EUPHRATES	C/173	Bombard railway and dugouts from B.4.d.60.20. - B.4.d.42.31.
	B/173	Bombard railway and dugouts from B.4.d.42.31. - B.4.d. 20.50
	D/173	Bombard railway and dugouts from B.4.d.60.20. - B.4.d.20.50.
	Ammunition	18 rounds per 18 pdr. battery 6 " " 4.5 How. "
TURNIP	B/173	Bombard both sides of mbank B.3.d.78.00. - B.4.c.10.50.
	C/173	Bombard trench B.3.d.78.00. - B.10.a.01.73.
	D/173	Bombard Dugouts B.4.c.05.25.
	Ammunition	24 rounds per 18 pdr. battery 12 " " 4.5 How. "
COLOGNE	C/173	Bombard Trench B.9.a.75.82. - B.9.a.65.90.
	B/173	" " B.9.a.75.82. - B.9.a.78.95.
	D/173	" Dugouts B.9.a.80.88.
	Ammunition	24 rounds per 18 pdr. battery 12 " " 4.5 How "
MILL	C/173	Bombard Company Headquarters at B.8.a.5.9.
	B/173	" Dugouts at B.8.a.3.9.
	D/173	" Telephone exchange at B.2.c.5.1.
	Ammunition	24 rounds per 18 pdr. battery 12 " " 4.5 How "
PIRE ALLER	462 Battery	Bombard Trench B.8.b.50.10. - B.8.b.30.20.
	B/173	" " B.8.b.30.20. - B.8.b.50.32.
	D/173	" " and Dugouts B.8.b.80.30. - B.8.b.60.50.
	Ammunition	24 rounds per 18 pdr. battery 12 " " 4.5 How "
TAURUS	C/173	Bombard Trench B.12.a.82.32. - B.12.a.75.50.
	B/173	" " B.12.a.75.50. - B.12.a.65.62.
	D/173	3 guns on Trench Junction B.12.a.75.50. 2 " " Dugouts B.12.a.58.70.
	Ammunition	12 rounds per 18 pdr. battery 6 " " 4.5 How "
JUNCTION	C/173	Bombard Trench B.4.a.10.41. - B.3.b.95.45.
	B/173	" " B.3.b.82.39. - B.3.b.70.41.
	D/173	" Dugouts B.3.b.92.41.
	Ammunition	24 rounds per 18 pdr. battery 12 " " 4.5 How "

Capt. R.F.A.

App V

Serial Number	Target		Observed from
1.	Dugout	B.3.b.75.25	ARLOIN
2.	Company Headquarters	B.9.a.60.45.	
3.	Dugouts at	B.9.a.80.80.	
4.	Dugouts at	B.9.a.10.90.	
5.	Cross Roads (M.G.Dugouts etc)	B.10.a.40.13.	JEANNET
6.	Dugouts	B.3.b.97.72.	
7.	Dugouts	B.4.c.00.25.	
8.	Dugouts in railway	B.11.c.	
9.	Dugouts and work in railway	B.17.b.	JEANNET
10.	Wood	B.11.b.	JEANNET
11.	O.P. and M.G. Emplacement	B.9.c.92.75.	ARLOIN
12.	Work along railway in	B.11.a.	JEANNET
13.	Company Headquarters	B.10.b.00.90.	
14.	T.M.	B.8.b.75.46.	ARLOIN
15.	O.P.	B.8.b.63.19.	SAULNIER
16.	O.P.	B.8.a.72.40.	ARLOIN
17.	O.P.	B.9.c.30.60.	
18.	O.P.	B.11.d.50.45.	JEANNET
19.	O.P.	B.8.d.73.97.	ARLOIN
20.	T.M.	B.9.a.00.98.	
21.	Dugouts	B.9.a.30.45.	
22.	M.G. Emplacement	B.9.c.07.83.	ARLOIN
23.	M.G. Emplacement	B.9.d.38.82.	ARLOIN
24.	M.G. Emplacement	B.8.b.95.00.	SAULNIER
25.	M.G. Emplacement	B.11.b.80.10.	JEANNET
26.	Battalion Headquarters	T.28.c.90.70.	
27.	Dump at	B.3.b.50.90.	
28.	Junction of Road and Railway	B.3.b.90.40.	

SECRET   173rd Brigade No. D.F.2.

```
O. C.  A/173
       B/173
       C/173
       D/173
       462 Battery R.F.A.
H.Q.   36th Div. Arty.
       107th Infy. Bde.
       108th Infy. Bde.
```

The following additional list of Targets is forwarded.

These are to be added to the list sent out under my No. D.F.1. of the 6th inst.

Serial Number	Target		Observed from
29.	Dugouts on Road	B.11.a.6.2.	JEANNET
30.	Listening Post	B.10.b.62.50.	JEANNET
31.	Dugouts	B.5.d.05.86.	
32.	Dugouts in Railway	B.1.d.0.3.	
33.	Dugouts	B.3.d.70.45.	
34.	Company Headquarters	P10.a.00.70.	
35.	Dugouts	B.3.d.90.20.	
36.	Track beside Bank	B.4.c.00.58. to B.9.b.25.35.	

8. 3. 18.

Captain R.F.A.
Adjutant RIGHT GROUP R.F.A.

SECRET

173rd Brigade No. D116/22

O.C.   A/173
          B/173
          C/173
          D/173
          482 Battery R.F.A.
H.Q. 107th Infy. Bde.
          108th Infy. Bde.

      Owing to the probability of the enemy being able to launch their attack before the Artillery Barrage comes down it has been decided to have a second barrage which will be just clear of the Line of Resistance.

      The method of procedure will be as follows:-

      On receipt of S.O.S. Signal all batteries will open fire on their present normal S.O.S. Lines.

      After 3 minutes their barrage will be lifted back to the line shown in attached.

      The barrage will remain here till further orders are received from Group Headquarters.

      This procedure will only obtain after the order "Man Battle Stations" has been issued.

      A further barrage which will be called for by a special signal and which will be designed to cover the line of redoubts will be issued in due course.

                                          Captain R.F.A.
                                Adjutant RIGHT GROUP   R.F.A.

11. 3. 18.

BARRAGE TO COVERLINE OF RESISTANCE

C/173
R.17.c.10.40.
R.17.c.25.42.
R.17.c.04.56.
R.16.d.98.64.
R.16.d.69.72.
R.16.d.56.80.

A/173
R.9.d.60.30.
R.9.d.40.30.
R.9.d.20.30.
R.9.d.08.30.
R.9.c.90.30.
R.4.c.95.29.

B/173
R.10.c.60.55.
R.10.c.40.33.
R.10.c.20.21.
R.10.c.09.10.
R.9.d. 90.40.
R.9.d. 75.45.

D/173
R.9.c.50.30.
R.9.c.35.25.
R.9.c.15.20.
R.9.c.05.30.
R.8.d.90.35.
R.8.d.70.35.

452 Battery R.F.A.
R.8.d.55.35.
R.8.d. 40.30.
R.8.d.25.30.
R.8.d.15.30.
R.8.d.05.40.
R.8.c.95.30.

The above settings give the centre of the zone for each gun. Guns will sweep to cover the intervening space. The necessary sweep will be worked out and will be arranged beforehand.

SECRET

O.C. /173

173rd Brigade No. D 116/25

App VII

The undermentioned barrage is intended to meet the situation which may arise if the Line of Resistance is broken by an enemy attack.

It will be fired for the defence of the two forward strong points in B.14.a. and B.16.c.

A tracing will be forwarded as soon as possible showing the barrage and also the position of the above forward points and the Machine guns.

The barrage will be ordered by Forward Observing Officer in JENNE D'ARC (B.19.d.98.40.) or ASCOT A.18.d.05.20. and Officers Commanding "B" and "D" Batteries 173rd Brigade will instruct their F.O.O's. accordingly.

```
A/173            B.14.d.84.93.  -  B.14.b.18.40.
462 Battery R.F.A. B.14.b.18.40.  -  B.14.b.00.82.
B/173            B.14.b.00.82.  -  B.8.c. 69.05.
C/173            B.8.c. 69.05.  -  B.8.c. 15.05.
D/173            B.16.a.47.15.  -  B.15.d.92.87.
```

11. 3. 18.

Capt. R.F.A.
Adjutant RIGHT GROUP R.F.A.

SECRET.   173rd Brigade R.F.A. No. W.P.51/12

O.C. A, B, C, and D/173
O.C. 383, 462, 463, and 464 Batteries.
C/Lieut Fagan R.E.

WORKING PARTIES.

A new position has now to be worked on and this necessitates reducing the number of shifts working at S.P.4. O.P. and S.P.5. O.P. O.P. at RAPHANEL will remain as before.

Work will now be as follows :-

POSITION.	BATTERY IN CHARGE.	R.E.	GROUP WORK-ING PARTY.	DETAILED BY.	MINERS.	DETAILED BY.
F 3.	464.	2	40.	(10 A/173.) (10 B/173.) (14 383) (6 462)	5	(4 A/173 (1 D/173
F 6.	383.	2	-	-	3	383.
F 4.	C/173.	-	-	-	-	-
F 7.	462.	2	-	-	3	462.
F 11.	B/173.	-	-	-	-	-
F 31.	D/173.	2	7	D/173.	-	-
F 28.	D/232.	-	10.	D/232.	-	-
F 23.	463.	-	-	-	3	463.
F 5.	A/173.	2	-	-	2	A/173.
O.P. S.P.4.	C/173.	-	14.	C/173.	6	C/173.
O.P. S.P.5.	D/173.	4	10.	D/173.	4	B/173.
O.P. RAPHANEL.	462.	4	16.	(10 462.) (6 D/232)	2	D/173.
O.P. DALLON.	463.	4	10.	(5 463.) (5 D/232)	-	-

Three shifts will be worked at O.P. RAPHANEL.
Two   "   "   "   "   "   "   S.P.4. S.P.5. and DALLON.

Work will be pushed on with the utmost energy.

The above arrangement will leave 25 men for work in the Battle Zone positions. These men are as follows :-

               A/173.   4.
               B/173.   6.
               C/173.   Nil.
               D/173.   Nil.
               463.   12.
               462.   Nil.
               383.   3.
               D/232.   Nil.
                          25.

12th February 1918.

Captain, R.F.A.,
Adjutant, RIGHT GROUP, R.F.A.

SECRET   173rd Brigade No.116/29

                                                 App. XI IX

O.C.   A/173
         B/173
         C/173
         D/173
         465 Battery R.F.A.
         494   "   "
H.Q.   107th Infy. Bde. }
         108th   "   "   } For information

            Herewith Barrage Tables showing :-
    (a) Barrage to be put down for the Defence of the Strong Points
in the Forward Zone in response to the special RED SMOKE S.O.S.
Signal.
            This Barrage will also be called for from the Strong
Points by telephone and the Officers Commanding B/173 and D/173
will satisfy themselves that the necessary communication is
arranged. (Visual will also be arranged if possible)
            They should also arrange that their F.O.O. knows
exactly where the Smoke Signal is to be sent from so that no delay
occurs in passing on the warning.
            The above batteries are responsible for passing on the
warning and informing Group Headquarters.
            If this Barrage is called for from any one strong point
the barrage on either side of that strong point will be put down.
            If more than one strong point demands the barrage the
whole barrage will be put down.

    (b) The Normal S.O.S. Lines for the defence of the Battle Zone
in the event of the forward zone being evacuated.

                                              [signature]
13.3.18.
                                              Captain R.F.A.
                                         Adjutant RIGHT GROUP R.F.A.

SECRET.
                                              173rd Brigade R.F.A. No.S.3/116/8

O.C. A/173.
     B/173.
     C/173.
     D/173.
     462 Battery R.F.A.,
(2) H.Q. 36th Divl. Artillery.
H.Q. 107th Inf. Brigade.
H.Q. 108th Inf. Brigade.
H.Q. Left Group, R.F.A.,

    It has been decided to bring the Normal S.O.S. Barrage nearer to our Outpost Line.

    From receipt of this Order your S.O.S. Lines will therefore be as shewn on the attached.

    Acknowledge by wire at once, please.

Issued at 10.30 p.m.
7th March 1918.
                                              Captain, R.F.A.,
                                    Adjutant, RIGHT GROUP, R.F.A.

RIGHT GROUP.

NORMAL S.O.S. LINES.

A/173 Brigade R.F.A.

B.9.d.65.48.
B.9.d.50.49.
B.9.d.35.50.
B.9.d.20.51.
B.9.d.65.52.
B.9.c.90.53.

C/173 Brigade R.F.A.

B.17.c.95.75.
B.17.c.84.90.
B.17.a.73.05.
B.17.a.62.20.
B.17.a.57.35.
B.17.a.40.50.

B/173 Brigade R.F.A.

B.10.c.50.70.
B.10.c.36.66.
B.10.c.22.62.
B.10.c.08.58.
B.9.d.94.52.
B.9.d.80.48.

462 Battery R.F.A.

B.8.d.90.45.
B.8.d.75.43.
B.8.d.60.41.
B.8.d.45.40.
B.8.d.30.55.
B.8.d.15.70.

D/173 Brigade R.F.A.

B.9.c.80.65.
B.9.c.64.64.
B.9.c.48.63.
B.9.c.33.62.
B.9.c.16.61.
B.9.c.00.60.

---oOo---

Secret   App. X

    O. C.   A/173   173rd Brigade No.
             B/173
             C/173
             D/173
             462 Battery R.F.A.
             464 Battery R.F.A.
    H.Q.   107th Infy. Bde.)
             108th "   "   ) For information
             36th Div. Arty.   )
    O. C.   Left Group

         Herewith Barrage Tables for :-

         A.   Mutual Support to Left Group

         B.   In case of attack on Right Sub Sector (held by 108th)
                                                    (Infy. Bde.   )
         C.   In case of attack on Centre Sub Sector(held by 107th)
                                                    (Infy. Bde.   )

         In all cases the necessary sweep should be calculated and
    arranged so that the whole front is covered equally.

                                                    [signature]
    13.5.18.   Captain R.F.A.
                                              Adjutant RIGHT GROUP R.F.A.

INTER-GROUP REINFORCING BARRAGES.

IN CASE OF ATTACK ON FRONT HELD BY 107th INF. BRIGADE.

CODE-WORD - "BERTHA".

B/173rd Brigade R.F.A.

B.10.c.77.45.
B.10.c.50.45.
B.10.c.20.45.
B.9.d.90.45.
B.9.d.70.50.
B.9.d.64.60.

C/173rd Brigade R.F.A.

B.10.c.35.45.
B.10.c.05.45.
B.9.d.80.48.
B.9.d.56.60.
B.9.d.40.60.
B.9.d.02.60.

A/173rd Brigade R.F.A.

B.9.d.48.60.
B.9.d.30.60.
B.9.d.19.60.
B.9.c.94.60.
B.9.c.80.70.
B.9.c.63.75.

462 Battery R.F.A.

B.9.c.47.74.
B.9.c.30.70.
B.9.c.13.66.
B.8.d.96.62.
B.8.d.79.58.
B.8.d.62.54.

464 Battery R.F.A.

B.8.d.45.50.
B.8.d.34.55.
B.8.d.24.62.
B.8.d.12.72.
B.8.d.02.75.
B.8.c.92.80.

D/173rd Brigade R.F.A.

B.10.d.20.20.
B.10.d.10.30.
B.10.d.00.40.
B.10.c.90.50.
B.10.c.80.60.
B.10.c.70.70.

1 18-pdr. Battery LEFT GROUP.

B.9.c.88.68.
B.9.c.70.73.
B.9.c.55.75.
B.9.c.38.72.
B.9.c.22.68.
B.9.c.04.64.

1 18-pdr. Battery LEFT GROUP.

B.8.d.88.60.
B.8.d.70.56.
B.8.d.54.52.
B.8.d.18.67.
B.8.d.07.74.
B.8.c.97.78.

1 Howitzer Battery, LEFT GROUP.

2 Guns on Cross Roads, B.8.b.30.30.
2 " " Trench Junction, B.8.b.72.59.
2 " " Trench Junction B.2.d.90.10.

INTER-GROUP REINFORCING BARRAGES.

IN CASE OF ATTACK ON FRONT HELD BY 108th INF. BRIGADE.

CODE-WORD "A N N A".

C/173rd Brigade R.F.A.,

    B.17.c.93.75.
    B.17.c.84.90.
    B.17.a.75.05.
    B.17.a.62.20.
    B.17.a.50.35.
    B.17.a.40.50.

A/173rd Brigade R.F.A.,

    B.17.c.77.97.
    B.17.a.56.27.
    B.17.a.35.50.
    B.17.a.25.51.
    B.17.a.15.53.
    B.17.a.05.55.

B/173rd Brigade R.F.A.,

    B.17.a.30.50.
    B.17.a.20.52.
    B.17.a.10.54.
    B.17.a.00.56.
    B.16.b.90.58.
    B.16.b.80.60.

464 Battery R.F.A.,

    B.16.b.95.57.
    B.16.b.85.59.
    B.16.b.75.63.
    B.16.b.67.68.
    B.16.b.61.75.
    B.16.b.49.90.

462 Battery R.F.A.,

    B.16.b.70.65.
    B.16.b.64.72.
    B.16.b.58.79.
    B.16.b.52.86.
    B.16.b.46.93.
    B.10.d.40.00.

D/173rd Brigade R.F.A.,

    B.10.d.20.20.
    B.10.d.10.30.
    B.10.d.00.40.
    B.10.c.90.50.
    B.10.c.80.60.
    B.10.c.70.70.

LEFT GROUP.   1 18-pdr. Battery B.10.d.60.70. to B.10.a.40.00.

-------oOo-------

RIGHT GROUP.

MUTUAL SUPPORT.

Help to LEFT GROUP.

    Code Word   "Help EDWARDES"

C/173	B.8.b.32.00. B.8.b.20.04. B.8.b.14.07. B.8.b.02.12. B.8.a.90.17. B.8.a.84.20.	A/173.	B.8.b.26.02. B.8.b.08.10. B.8.a.96.14. B.8.a.78.22. B.8.a.66.26. B.8.a.48.34.
B/173	B.8.a.72.24. B.8.a.60.29. B.8.a.54.32. B.8.a.42.36. B.8.a.30.42. B.8.a.24.44.	464 Bty RFA.	B.8.a.36.39. B.8.a.18.46. B.8.a.06.52. B.8.a.88.60. B.8.a.76.64. B.8.a.58.70.
462 Bty R.F.A.	B.8.a.12.49. B.8.a.00.55. B.7.b.94.58. B.7.b.82.62. B.7.b.70.66. B.7.b.64.68.	D/173	1 How. on B.1.d.7.1. 1 How on B.2.c.1.8. 1 How on B.2.c.20.32 1 How on B.2.c.75.48 1 How on B.2.d.63.63. 1 How on B.8.b.30.40.

SECRET.   173rd Brigade R.F.A No. M75/13

O.C. C/173
     D/173.

App. XI

With reference to the withdrawal of your three Guns which is taking place to-night.

1. The rear half Battery will not fire except for the minimum number of rounds necessary for Registration. When this is being carried out the forward half Battery must provide covering fire under Battery arrangements.

2. The forward half Batteries will carry out the present programme of firing, including wire cutting, and Battery Commanders will make the necessary arrangements for strengthening the Detachments.

3. There will be no detached Guns when the move is complete.

4. The Headquarters of Batteries will move with the rear half Battery, and all necessary extensions to the present communications will be made so that the rear half Battery can function independently.

5. The establishment of ammunition remains the same, i.e. 676 rounds per 18-pdr gun, and 508 rounds per 4.5 How at both forward and rear positions. Rear positions must be complete with this amount by dawn 18th.

                                        Captain R.F.A.
                                Adjutant 173rd Brigade R.F.A.

17.3.18.

SECRET AND URGENT.   173rd Brigade R.F.A. No. B19

O.C. A/173
      B/173
      C/173
      C/173 Forward position
      D/173
      D/173 Forward position
      464 Battery R.F.A.

App XII

    Barrage in accordance with the attached Table will be fired to-night at 8.30 p.m.

    18-pdrs will fire 50% "A" and 50% "AX" (except where range is excessive). 4.5 Hows will fire 25% 106 fuzes.

    Rate of fire for guns and hows as fast as is consistent with accurate shooting, not exceeding four rounds per gun per minute.

    Please acknowledge by wire.

19.3.18.

Capt R.F.A.
Adjutant RIGHT GROUP R.F.A.

BARRAGE TABLE.

BATTERY.	TIME.	TASK.
B/173.	Zero to Zero plus 3 Minutes.	B.9.b.75.00. – B.10.a.15.10.
	Zero plus 3 Minutes to Zero plus 6 Minutes.	B.9.b.70.15. – B.10.a.13.23.
	Zero plus 6 minutes to Zero plus 9 minutes.	B.9.b.68.35. – B.10.a.10.40.
	Zero plus 9 minutes to Zero plus 12 minutes.	B.9.b.60.50. – B.10.a.05.60.
	Zero plus 12 minutes to Zero plus 15 minutes.	B.9.b.60.60. – B.10.a.05.75.

A/173.   Same as B/173.
D/173. Rear Guns.   Same as B/173.
C/173. Forward Guns.

	Zero to Zero plus 3 minutes.	B.10.a.15.10. – B.10.a.40.13.
	" plus 3 minutes to Zero plus 6 minutes.	B.10.a.13.23. – B.10.a.40.30.
	" plus 6 minutes to Zero plus 9 minutes.	B.10.a.10.40. – B.10.a.35.47.
	" plus 9 minutes to Zero plus 12 minutes.	B.10.a.05.60. – B.10.a.30.60.
	" plus 12 minutes to Zero plus 15 minutes.	B.10.a.05.75. – B.10.a.30.80.

C/173. Rear Guns.   Same as C/173. Forward Guns.
D/173. Forward Guns.

	Zero to Zero plus 3 Minutes.	B.10.a.40.13. – B.10.a.55.15.
	" plus 3 minutes to Zero plus 6 minutes.	B.10.a.40.30. – B.10.a.55.33.
	" plus 6 minutes to Zero plus 9 minutes.	B.10.a.35.47. – B.10.a.50.50.
	" plus 9 minutes to Zero plus 12 minutes.	B.10.a.30.60. – B.10.a.48.63.
	" plus 12 minutes to Zero plus 15 minutes.	B.10.a.30.80. – B.10.a.45.75.

464. 2 Guns. Same as D/173. Forward Guns.

RIGHT GROUP   36th DIVISIONAL ARTILLERY

Account of Operations   March 21st - 31st.

Reference Map FRANCE
Sheet 66 c 1/40,000

Reliable information having been obtained from deserters that the Enemy attack would take place on the morning of the 21st March a Programme of vigorous Counter Preparation was ordered for the night 20/21st. Suspected Trench Mortar Emplacements were especially dealt with, and weaving barrages fire on selected areas.

Between 10.30. p.m. and 12 midnight all remaining batteries were withdrawn to positions behind the Battle Zone, B/173 to A.27.a. C/173 to G.6.c., and D/173 to G.4.b.   Practically all ammunition was removed from the Forward Positions, or fired before they were evacuated. From information received later through F.O.O's it is certain that had Batteries remained in Forward Positions they would have been annihilated without having been able to take any active part in the Battle. Group Headquarters had been moved the previous day to G.3.a.

The Enemy Barrage opened at 4.35 a.m. while Counter Preparations was actually being fired. During the first 5 minutes telephonic communication was destroyed to all batteries with the exception of the 464th Battery in G.5.c., who remained in communication for about 20 minutes.

heavy
Owing to an exceptionally/mist and to the lack of all communication it is extremely difficult to give a detailed account of the Enemy Barrage. As far as can be ascertained it appeared to consist of :- 1. A Barrage by Trench Mortars of all calibres on the Forward System, 2. A mixed Phosgene and H.E. Bombardment by 105, 150 and 210 M.M. shell directed against A The Line of Strong Points and the Valley immediately in rear, B The Battle Line, and C The Valley extending from G.3.a. to ESSIGNY STATION. This Barrage was especially heavy on Battery Positions. The proportion of Lethal Shell to H.E. gradually decreased, until the Barrage was entirely composed of H.E. There was a remarkable absence of 77 m.m. shell, and of instantaneous fuze. 3 A Bombardment of selected points by H.V. Guns of all calibres. These points included almost all villages within range, the canal crossings, and the R.E. Dump near GRAND SERAUCOURT.   A Howitzer of very heavy calibre was also noticed firing intermittently on some area near the canal S.W. of GRAND SERAUCOURT.

Finding that communications to the rear were interupted Batteries immediately opened fire on their S.O.S. Lines. The presence of Gas in strong concentration necessitating the wearing of Box Respirators and the mist which completely obscured aiming posts, rendered it very difficult to keep up a steady rate of accurate fire.

Every effort to restore communication with batteries was made. It was found however that all buried routes had been cut, and the barrage was so heavy that no air line could have survived. At 6 a.m. a party consisting of 2 Officers and 4 O.R's went forward to endeavour to obtain some information. They walked through an intense barrage, one of the party being wounded, and got into touch with batteries in the neighbourhood of G.4.b.   They were unable to obtain any information owing to the mist.

At about 10 a.m. orders were sent to batteries by runners that until information was received that an attack had been launched Counter Preparation Targets must be engaged, the rate of fire being adjusted in accordance with the amount of ammunition in hand. Meanwhile every effort was made to replenish the ammunition supply and later in the morning it was found possible to get ammunition through to all batteries at the expense of some casualties.

At 11 a.m. orders were sent out to batteries to put down a Barrage on the Line of Strong Points.

At 12 noon information was received that the enemy was advancing in the neighbourhood of LA MANUFACTURE FARM. Orders were therefore issued to the batteries near ESSIGNY STATION to retire by Sections, and the Gun Limbers which had rendezvoused in G.14. were ordered up to the Positions. By this time the enemy barrage had ceased, but there was still a good deal of intermittent fire in G.8. and 9. The mist too had cleared.

At this time the enemy appears to have advanced very rapidly towards ESSIGNY STATION, being reported on the Railway in G.6.a. at 12.45.p.m. and in G.12.b. at 1.10. p.m. He seems to have been advancing in two parties, one moving South along the Railway and the other West from the direction of ESSIGNY. The Limbers sent up to the Batteries near ESSIGNY STATION were turned back by the retiring Infantry in G.10.a. A further attempt was made to reach these positions at 2.15.p.m. but it was found to be impossible.

At 1.15.p.m. C/173 and A/173 in action in G.6.c. and G.5.d. respectively withdrew their personnel from their positions as they were then under heavy machine gun fire from front flank and rear and the enemy was seen to be advancing rapidly from ESSIGNY.

Much of the information given above did not reach Group Headquarters until very much later, and at 2.0. p.m. the situation, so far as the Infantry Brigadier and Group Commander knew, was very vague. Unreliable reports from stragglers stated that the enemy was through the Battle Zone at all points and had captured POURGIES FARM. A reconnaisance was immediately ordered by the Group Commander to go forward and ascertain the situation. They reported that the enemy was holding ESSIGNY STATION and was in B.11.b. and that our Infantry were holding a line in A27.d. in some strength, also that our Batteries were still in action in G.4.b. and G.5.c. though exposed to Machine Gun fire.

The situation remained more or less unchanged throughout the afternoon. The remaining 18 pdr. batteries being withdrawn from G.5.c. at various times D/173 remained in action in G.4.b. until 6 p.m. This Battery sent forward an F.O.O. to the copse at A.28.d.0.2. and maintained communication with him, bringing observed fire to bear on enemy advancing at ranges down to 800 yards. They finally withdrew all their guns safely at 6 p.m. having expended practically all their ammunition, and took up a position in G.15.b.

At 7.15.p.m. the enemy was reported to be advancing in G.4.b. and G.5.a. By 7.45 p.m. he was in G.4.c. and G.3.d. All batteries remaining in action were consequently ordered to withdraw to positions near ARTEMPS, coming under orders of Officer Commanding 153 Brigade R.F.A. 173 Brigade H.Q. withdrew at the same time to OLLEZY.

From March 22nd to 31st D/173 was the only Battery of the Brigade remaining in action. The other 3 Batteries came under the orders of O.C. 36th D.A.C. and were used to assist in ammunition supply, also a large number of their Officers, men and horses were drafted to fill vacancies in Batteries in the line. A, B, and C batteries retired as follows:

On the night of the 21st they were at SOMMETTE EAUCOURT moving on the morning of the 22nd to VERLAINES and the same afternoon to GOLANCOURT. Thence on the 23rd to AVRICOURT and on the night of the 25th to FRESNERES. On the 25th they were at

GRVILLERS, moving the same evening to PIENNES. On the 27th they moved to MERY, on the 28th to GOURNAY, on the night 30/31 to GRAND FRESNOY and on the 31st to LA RUE ST PIERRE.

D/173 remained in the line. An account of the activities of this Battery is attached.

So little information was received at Group Headquarters at the time that it is difficult to obtain a connected account of the operations on the day of the original attack. Separate accounts by Battery Commanders are therefore attached.

Appendix 13

Immediately follows War Diary.

36th Divisional Artillery.

173rd BRIGADE R.F.A. :::: APRIL 1918.

April 1918.

173rd Brigade R.F.A. Army Form C. 2118.
36th Division
II Corps. Second Army.

WAR DIARY
or
INTELLIGENCE SUMMARY.
(Erase heading not required.)

Place	Date	Hour	Summary of Events and Information	Remarks and references to Appendices
				Ref. maps. Cambrai 1/100000 Belgium, Sheets 27, 28 1/40,000
	1st		The Brigade, less D/173, remained at LA RUE ST. PIERRE.	
	2nd		marched to FRANCASTEL.	
	3rd		marched to OFFIGNIES in the POIX collecting area.	
	4th		D/173 rejoined the Brigade	
	5th 6th 7th		The Brigade remained at OFFIGNIES. Re-organization and refitting work was carried out. The Brigade was completed in guns, and a good deal of other equipment was supplied	
	8th		The Brigade marched to COURCELLES SUR POIX.	
	9th 10th		Brigade remained at COURCELLES SUR POIX, and the work of refitting was carried on.	
	11th		The Brigade marched to PONT DE METZ.	
	12th 13th		The Brigade remained at PONT DE METZ	
	14th		The Brigade entrained at St ROCH Station near AMIENS.	
	15th		The Brigade detrained at HOPOUTRE near POPERINGHE, and marched to wagon lines near MONT DE CATS.	
	16th		Nothing unusual occurred.	

Army Form C. 2118.

April (cont.)

WAR DIARY
or
INTELLIGENCE SUMMARY.
(Erase heading not required.)

Instructions regarding War Diaries and Intelligence Summaries are contained in F.S. Regs., Part II. and the Staff Manual respectively. Title pages will be prepared in manuscript.

Place	Date	Hour	Summary of Events and Information	Remarks and references to Appendices
	17th		A/173, B/173 and D/173 moved into action in the neighbourhood of BERTHEN, with Group Headquarters at Sheet 27, R21.b.3.2, coming under the orders of 38th Divisional Artillery and covering the 34th Division.	
	18th		C/173 remained at its Wagonline, as its equipment had been drawn on to equip other Batteries. Battery Wagon Lines moved to neighbourhood of BOESCHEPE. The attitude of the enemy was fairly quiet. Our Artillery however assumed a most aggressive policy, 60 rounds per Battery per hour being fired into the enemy's forward areas.	
	19th		The weather became dull and cold and some snow fell. During the early morning a concentrated gas bombardment was carried out by four 4.5" Hows. against BAILLEUL ASYLUM. During the afternoon enemy artillery showed greater activity, carrying out sudden heavy bombardments on selected areas at different times. Nothing unusual occurred.	
	20th to 22nd		Nothing unusual occurred.	
	23rd		During this period the British Infantry was relieved by the French. The Brigade moved out of action, spending the night at Wagon Lines near GODEWAERSVELDE. The relief was delayed for some hours by a heavy enemy Artillery bombardment at 8 pm followed by an Infantry attack which was repulsed.	

Army Form C. 2118.

WAR DIARY
or
INTELLIGENCE SUMMARY.
(Erase heading not required.)

Instructions regarding War Diaries and Intelligence Summaries are contained in F. S. Regs., Part II. and the Staff Manual respectively. Title pages will be prepared in manuscript.

April (cont?)

Place	Date	Hour	Summary of Events and Information	Remarks and references to Appendices
	24th		The Brigade moved to HAMHOEK.	
	25th		The Brigade moved to the neighbourhood of BRIELEN	
	26th		The Brigade moved to Wagon Lines in the neighbourhood Sheet 28, B 20.d.	
	27th		Batteries took up reserve positions in Sheet 28, B 19, to cover the Canal Line. From 9-30 a.m. to 5. p.m the enemy carried out a sustained and heavy bombardment of our back areas with 240 m.m. and 150 m.m. high velocity guns. This shelling was particularly severe in the neighbourhood of the Batteries, where heavy casualties were caused among men and horses, principally from 240 m.m. Shell bursting on time. Casualties of the Brigade were 1 officer died of wounds 2 officers wounded 4 O.R's Killed 24 O.R's wounded 19 horses killed.	
	28th		During the night Brigade Headquarters moved to HOSPITAL FARM. Brigade moved into action in Sheet 28, B 24, Headquarters being at C. 25. d. 1.7.	

Army Form C. 2118.

WAR DIARY
or
INTELLIGENCE SUMMARY.

(Erase heading not required.)

April (cont'd)

Place	Date	Hour	Summary of Events and Information	Remarks and references to Appendices
	28th (cont'd)		During the night "B" and "D" Batteries moved to more rear positions in B.23. The attitude of the enemy on this front was unaggressive.	
	29th		Quiet day. Nothing unusual occurred.	
	30th		Officer Casualties during the month were as follows:—	
			Died of wounds. 2/Lt. J.L. MANN	
			Wounded Capt. F.J.M. HUNT	
			Lieut. H.M. ACHILLES	
			2/Lt. H. IDDON	
			2/Lt. E.M. CUNNINGHAM	

W.C.P.
Lieut. Col. R.F.A.
Commanding 173rd Bde R.F.A

Army Form C. 2118.

WAR DIARY
or
INTELLIGENCE SUMMARY.   173rd Brigade R.F.A.   36th Division

(Erase heading not required.)

MAY 1918.

Instructions regarding War Diaries and Intelligence Summaries are contained in F. S. Regs., Part II and the Staff Manual respectively. Title pages will be prepared in manuscript.

Place	Date	Hour	Summary of Events and Information	Remarks and references to Appendices
			As Left Group 36th Divisional Artillery the Brigade covered the front between KITCHENER WOOD and WIELTJE, with the Belgian army on the left, and Right Group 36th Divisional Artillery on the right.	Reference. 28. N.W. 1/20,000. and sheet 28 1/40,000.
			Throughout the month there has been a gradual decrease of hostile artillery activity. At the beginning of the month forward areas received considerable attention, whereas back areas were comparatively quiet.	
			Gradual moving forward of the enemy's batteries appears to have taken place with the result that back areas came under field artillery fire in proportion.	
			Shortly after the middle of the month this movement appears to have reached its climax, and hostile batteries were reported active from positions within a few thousand yards of our own front line, some of them to the WEST of the STEENBEKE. From then until the end of the month though the bulk of the enemy artillery undoubtedly remained to move forward these very forward batteries appear in most cases to have been withdrawn.	
			At the end of the month the area EAST of the Canal was very quiet indeed, whilst battery positions and roads to the WEST of the canal as far back as BRIELEN frequently came under heavy fire. Hostile gas shelling also showed a gradual decrease as the month	

WAR DIARY or INTELLIGENCE SUMMARY.

MAY 1918

progressed, practically none being reported during the last week although weather conditions were ideal.

Our Artillery carried out an active policy of harassing fire, at the beginning of the month the allotment of ammunition being 60 rds per battery per hour. Later this was reduced to 20 rds per battery per hour.

During the early part of the month counter-preparation shoots were frequently carried out at dusk and before dawn. These were discontinued when the likelihood of enemy attacks in this Sector disappeared.

Thanks to good visibility Zone calls on enemy batteries and transport were frequently received and answered, and several counter battery shoots with ground observation were carried out with 4.5" Hows. with great success. Gas bombardments were also undertaken whenever weather conditions were favourable.

The weather throughout the month was remarkably fine and dry.

Our casualties during the month were negligible.

Army Form C. 2118.

3.

WAR DIARY
or
INTELLIGENCE SUMMARY.

(Erase heading not required)

MAY 1918

Place	Date	Hour	Summary of Events and Information	Remarks and references to Appendices
	1st-4th		Nothing unusual occurred.	
	5		Enemy artillery very quiet.	
	6		"A" Battery 173rd Brigade R.F.A. was withdrawn to its Wagon Line to rest. "D" Battery moved 4 guns to a position EAST of the Canal C20.d.1.9. During the day the enemy showed increased activity against roads.	
	7		Normal.	
	8		Unusually clear visibility. Enemy high velocity guns more active	
	9		Normal	
	10		The front held by 104th Infantry Brigade was extended — see appendix 'A'.	App: 'A'
	11		A gas concentration was carried out in conjunction with the Right Group — see appendix B	App: B
	12, 13, 14		Normal	
	15		A gas concentration was carried out in conjunction with the Right Group. see appendix 'C'	App: 'C'
	16		Gas concentration was fired in conjunction with Right Group - see appendix 'D'	App: 'D'

Army Form C. 2118.

WAR DIARY
or
INTELLIGENCE SUMMARY.
(Erase heading not required.)

MAY 1918   4.

Place	Date	Hour	Summary of Events and Information	Remarks and references to Appendices
	17		Normal	
	18		Gas concentration fired in conjunction with Right Group – see appendix E	App: E
	19/20		Normal	
	21		Gas concentration fired in conjunction with Right Group – see appendix F	App: F
	22			
	23		Normal.	
	24			
	25		Gas concentration fired in conjunction with Right Group – see appendix G.	App. G
	26		Normal	
	27		A minor operation was carried out by the 108th Brigade, with Artillery co-operation by both Groups – see appendix 'H'.	App. H.
	28		Gas concentration fired in conjunction with Right Group – see appendix I	App. I
	29/30		Normal.	
	31		A minor operation was carried out by the 108th Infantry Brigade. An Artillery programme was arranged and held in readiness should it be called for. As the raiding party met with no opposition, the Artillery did not open fire. (See appendix K.)	App. K

A 5834. Wt. W4973/M687 730,000 8/16 D.D. & L. Ltd. Forms/C.2118/13.

Army Form C. 2118.

WAR DIARY
or
INTELLIGENCE SUMMARY.

(Erase heading not required.)

MAY 1918.

Place	Date	Hour	Summary of Events and Information	Remarks and references to Appendices
			The Units of the Brigade were located as follows:-	

Unit	Position	Wagon Lines	First Wagon Lines
Headquarters 173 Bde R.F.A.	C.25.d.00.85	N° 6 PESELHOEK STDGS.	A.21.b.2.9
A/173 Battery	C.19.c.65.30	A.14.b.4.7	B.21.b.40.75
B/173	{B.24.a.2.2 (4 guns) C.20.a.9.2 (2 ")	A.14.b.9.3	B.21.d.9.8
C/173	{B.24.c.80.18 (4 guns) C.26.a.10.30 (2 ")	A.21.a.6.4	B.30.a.3.7
D/173	{C.20.d.10.90 (4 guns) B.23.c.50.58 (2 ")	A.21.b.2.9	B.21.d.4.6

Brigade and Battery Commanders etc. were as follows:-

Headquarters
Bt. Lt. Col. H.C. SIMPSON D.S.O.
Lt. (A/Capt) F.N. BROOME Adjutant
Lt. C. BOSTOCK SMITH R.E. Signal Officer
Lt. C.N. JESSOP, Orderly Officer

'A' Battery
2/Lt. (A/major) R.R. SHARP. D.S.O. M.C.
2/Lt. (A/capt) T.H. SHEARER. M.C

B. Battery
Capt (A/major) R.C. EMPSON
Lt. (A/ capt) A.G. SHIRRA GIBB

C. Battery
Capt (A/major) G.W. LEE
Capt. W. ARNOLD

D. Battery
Lt. (A/major) R.P. SCHWEDER. M.C
Lt. J. CLAYTON HARDIE.

Lieut Col
R.F.A.

Commanding 173rd Bde R.F.A.

WAR DIARY or INTELLIGENCE SUMMARY

173rd Brigade R.F.A.
36th Division
II Corps

June 1918.

Army Form C. 2118.

Place	Date	Hour	Summary of Events and Information	Remarks and references to Appendices
			Reference 28/N.W/1/20,000 28/1/40,000.	

As Left Group 36th Divisional Artillery the Brigade covered the front between KITCHENER WOOD and WIELTJE, with the Belgian Army on the Left, and Right Group 36th Divisional Artillery on the Right.

On the nights 5/6 and 6/7 June the Brigade was relieved by the Artillery of the 12th Belgian Division – I/12 A. and III/12 A.

During the few days the Brigade was in action the gradual decrease of Hostile Artillery activity was maintained. The area East of the Canal was very quiet indeed but Battery Positions in roads to the West of the Canal as far back as BRIELEN frequently came under heavy fire.

Hostile gas shelling was slight.

Our Artillery carried out an active policy of harassing fire, the allotment of ammunition being 18-pdr. 25 rds. per Battery per hour and 4.5" Hows. 15 rds. per Battery per hour.

Army Form C. 2118.

WAR DIARY
or
INTELLIGENCE SUMMARY.
(Erase heading not required.)

173 Bde R.F.A. (contd)

June 1918.

Place	Date	Hour	Summary of Events and Information	Remarks and references to Appendices
			A Gas Concentration took place on the night 4/5th June. Zone calls on enemy Batteries and Transport were received and answered, and a "Counter Battery shoot" with ground observation was carried out with 4.5" Hows. On relief the Brigade proceeded to Clifford Camp and remained there for the rest of the month. A Training Programme was carried through each week. On the 9th June the Brigade was inspected by the G.O.C Second Army. The Brigade suffered from an epidemic of Influenza during the month, the sick returns in the middle of the month being over 200. By methods of segregation the outbreak was brought under with success, and the sick returns at the end of the month were only slightly more than normal. The weather throughout the month was remarkably fine and dry. Our Casualties during the month were negligible.	

Army Form C. 2118.

WAR DIARY
or
INTELLIGENCE SUMMARY.

173 Bde R.F.A. (Cont?) June 1918

(Erase heading not required.)

Instructions regarding War Diaries and Intelligence Summaries are contained in F.S. Regs., Part II. and the Staff Manual respectively. Title pages will be prepared in manuscript.

Place	Date	Hour	Summary of Events and Information	Remarks and references to Appendices
June	1-3		Battery Positions were made on the BLUE LINE and O.P's were reconnoitred. One Section per Battery 18-pdrs went into action on the evening of the 11th June with a dump of 100 rounds per Gun, and one Section of 4.5" Hows. on the evening of the 12th. Detachments of 1 N.C.O. and 2 men remained with the guns.	
	4.		The Brigade also built on the 28th June similar positions on the BLUE LINE for the four Batteries of the 246th Brigade R.F.A.	
	5-6		Enemy Artillery very quiet.	
	6-7		A gas concentration was fired. Appendix I	App. I
	7		One Section per Battery relieved.	
			Remaining Sections of Batteries relieved.	
	9		Headquarters relieved. Moved to Clifford Camp. Inspection by G.O.C. II Army.	
	11		18-pdr Section per Battery moved into action on the BLUE LINE	

WAR DIARY

173 Bde R.F.A. (Cont)

June 1918

Place	Date	Hour	Summary of Events and Information	Remarks and references to Appendices
June	12		4.5" How. Section moved into Action on the BLUE LINE.	
	13-30		Occupied by Training Programme.	

H.R.
Lieut. Col. R.F.A.
Commanding 173 Bde R.F.A.

Army Form C. 2118.

WAR DIARY
or
INTELLIGENCE SUMMARY.
(Erase heading not required.)

173rd Brigade R.F.A
36th Division
Xth Corps. II Army.

JULY 1918

Place	Date	Hour	Summary of Events and Information	Remarks and references to Appendices
1.			The Brigade having finished its period of Rest and Training, left CLIFFORD CAMP on the 4th July, and proceeded to WEMMERS CAPPEL, and from there relieved the 11/4 R.A.C. of the 41st (French) Divisional Artillery in the ST. JANS CAPPEL Sector. The Relief was effected on the night 6th/7 and 7th/8th without incident The Brigade with the 40yth Battery A.F.A. now formed the RIGHT GROUP of the Divisional Artillery, and covered the Front from 27/SE x11d 3.6 to 28/SW. S.1.d.9.4. Liaison with the Infantry was maintained by a Subaltern Officer continuously at the Headquarters of the Battalion in the Line. Two Group O.Ps, "ANDRÉ" and "CLUB" were manned continuously night and day, while batteries manned forward O.Ps. by day. A Rocket Guard was established at PIEBROUCK. During the month a considerable amount of work was done on Battery positions, Command Posts being made in most cases and shelters for the men.	Ref. 27.SE & 28.SW. combined 1/20.000 27/40.000

Army Form C. 2118.

WAR DIARY
or
INTELLIGENCE SUMMARY.

(Erase heading not required.)

2.

Place	Date	Hour	Summary of Events and Information	Remarks and references to Appendices
173 Bde. R.F.A	JULY (Cont'd)		Hostile Artillery activity during the month has been gradually on the increase. This no doubt is partly owing to the activity and movement that the enemy can see in our lines, and also perhaps to the fact of his having had to postpone his attack. Battery positions have not been heavily shelled, the enemy appearing to confine himself mostly to Area shoots. He has used 77 mm guns from forward positions, especially about S.8.d and S.14.b. During the last few days of the month he did a considerable amount of gas shelling, consisting of bursts of fire from one or more batteries. Enemy Aircraft were fairly active, especially towards the end of the month. Our own Artillery carried out an active policy of harassing fire two-thirds of which took place during the night, and from forward positions. The amount of Ammunition allowed was 150 rounds per gun at the beginning of the month, which was increased to 200 rounds per gun. This harassing fire was carried out in conjunction with the Machine Guns of the Infantry Brigade and was directed on likely spots, especially roads and tracks used by the enemy infantry. Concentrations were also fired on many occasions.	

Army Form C. 2118.

WAR DIARY
or
INTELLIGENCE SUMMARY.
(Erase heading not required.)

173 Bde R.F.A

Instructions regarding War Diaries and Intelligence Summaries are contained in F. S. Regs., Part II. and the Staff Manual respectively. Title pages will be prepared in manuscript.

3. JULY (Cont^d)

Place	Date	Hour	Summary of Events and Information	Remarks and references to Appendices
			Gas concentrations were carried out by the 4.5" Hows on three occasions during the month.	
			The Group took part in the successful operation on METEREN by the 9th Division on Friday July 19th at 7.55 a.m., co-operating as left support.	
			The dumps of ammunition at the guns were finally increased to 750 rounds per gun 18-pdrs and 550 rounds per 4.5" Howitzer.	
			The weather during the early part of the month was fine and dry. Later a good deal of wet and some thunderstorms were experienced. Visibility was fair only. Wind mostly W. to S.W.	
			Casualties during the month amounted to 2 O.Rs killed and 2 O.Rs. wounded.	
	1st.		Divisional Horse Show.	
	4		The Brigade moved to WEMAERS CAPPEL.	
	6-7		The Brigade relieved the French (R.A.C. 41st Div.) in ST JANS CAPPEL Sector.	
	10.		Hostile Artillery active.	

WAR DIARY or INTELLIGENCE SUMMARY.

Army Form C. 2118.

173. Bde. R.F.A.

Place	Date	Hour	Summary of Events and Information	Remarks and references to Appendices
	JULY (Cont'd)			
	11.		Hostile artillery very quiet.	
	13.		Moved Group Headquarters to MONT DES CATS.	
	15.		Enemy barraged 1st and 2nd Support Lines of our Sector.	
	17.		Forward Sections being moved back. C/173 moved to rear position.	
	19.		Concentrations fired. 700 rounds per Battery between 10 pm & 3. am. Attack of the 9th Division on METEREN (see Appendix I)	app. I
	20.		Heavy artillery fire on our front line.	
	21.		The Brigade fired concentrations during the night, over 1000 rounds for the Brigade.	
	25.		Enemy Artillery active. Detached Sections move forward.	
	26.		Gas concentration fired at night by 4.5" How. Battery (see appendix II)	app. II
	29.		Enemy Artillery active.	
	30.		Enemy artillery active	
			Gas concentration fired by Brigade 4.5" How Battery. Simpson Group order No 4 see appendix III	appen. III

W.E.P.

Lt. Col. R.F.A.
Commanding SIMPSON GROUP R.F.A.

Army Form C. 2118.

WAR DIARY
or
INTELLIGENCE SUMMARY.

(Erase heading not required.)

173rd Brigade R.F.A.
36th Division
Xth Corps. Second Army

AUGUST 1918

Place	Date	Hour	Summary of Events and Information	Remarks and references to Appendices
			Ref. 27. SE. & 28. SW continued	20,000

The Brigade during the greater part of the month continued to cover the same Sector of Front, forming the Right Group of the Divisional Artillery. The same arrangements for O.Ps. Rocket Guards, etc, were kept up as in the preceding month.

The policy of doing all the harassing fire by the Forward Sections was continued. Battery positions were changed in most cases and a considerable amount of work was done in making Command Posts, and Shelters for the men.

Hostile Artillery activity during the month increased slightly, especially during the period in which the enemy was preparing to withdraw his lines. This took the form mostly of area shoots, and a considerable amount of gas shell was employed.

Enemy aircraft were fairly active.

Our Artillery carried out an active policy of harassing fire and concentrations, and several operations were undertaken by our own Infantry, and the Divisions on the Left and on the Right of us.

Army Form C. 2118.

WAR DIARY
or
INTELLIGENCE SUMMARY.
(Erase heading not required.)

Instructions regarding War Diaries and Intelligence Summaries are contained in F. S. Regs., Part II. and the Staff Manual respectively. Title pages will be prepared in manuscript.

173 Bde. R.F.A.

August 1918

Place	Date	Hour	Summary of Events and Information	Remarks and references to Appendices
			Lieut-Col. H.C. SIMPSON, D.S.O, R.F.A, was Commanding the Divisional Artillery from Monday 5th August until Wednesday 21st August and during that period the Group was commanded by Lieut-Col. NEVINSON. It became evident towards the end of the month that the enemy was withdrawing his guns, and keeping up considerable activity with very few Batteries. On the 30th of August the enemy withdrew and Batteries were ordered forward. The weather during the whole of the month was fine and dry. Visibility was fair only. Wind mostly WEST to SOUTH WEST. Casualties during the month were negligible.	
August	1st			
	2		Projector operation against MURAL FARM (see appendix I)	app. I
	4/5		Enemy shelled very heavily until 5.9s about 10.0 p.m.	
	6		Gas concentration fired on the Square Bailleul (see appendix II)	app. II
			Considerable enemy artillery activity.	
	9		Gas projector attack on MURAL FARM	
	10		Gas concentration fired on road junction S.14.d 35.82 (see appendix III) Considerable hostile Artillery activity on Battery areas.	app. III

Army Form C. 2118.

WAR DIARY
or
INTELLIGENCE SUMMARY.
(Erase heading not required.)

173 Bde R.F.A.

August 1918

Place	Date	Hour	Summary of Events and Information	Remarks and references to Appendices
	11		Considerable hostile Artillery activity.	
	12		Bombardment of SHODDY FARM by our Heavy Artillery, in which we co-operated. (see appendix IV)	App: IV
	13		Gas concentration fired on stream crossing S.13.d.05.65 to X.18.C.90.42 (see Appendix V)	App: V
			Gas concentration fired on enemy support companies billets in BAILLEUL (see appendix VI)	App VI
	14		Wire cut by hurricane bombardment	
			Battery positions reconnoitred for the "B" scheme.	
	16		Wire cut by hurricane bombardment (see appendix VII)	App: VII
	18		Raid on MURAL FARM (see appendix VIII)	App: VIII
	21/22		Operations by 30th Division, in which we co-operated, and carried out a chinese attack on WIRRAL FARM. (see appendix IX)	App. IX
	22		Counter attack by the enemy repulsed by our Artillery fire.	
	24		Attack by the 36th Division, both Battalions obtaining their objectives.	
	27		Col. H.C. SIMPSON, D.S.O. R.F.A. proceeded to Divisional Artillery Headquarters as C.R.A., Major R.R. SHARP commanding the Group.	

Army Form C. 2118.

WAR DIARY
or
INTELLIGENCE SUMMARY.

(Erase heading not required.)

173 Bde R.F.A

August 1918

Place	Date	Hour	Summary of Events and Information	Remarks and references to Appendices
	27		Enemy bombarded St. JANS CAPPEL heavily with Gas.	
	30		Batteries and Group Headquarters went forward to areas in M.31. and M.32.d.	
	31		Batteries moved forward to S.16.	

Major R.F.A.
Commanding SIMPSON GROUP, R.F.A.

Army Form C. 2118.

98/35

WAR DIARY or INTELLIGENCE SUMMARY.

(Erase heading not required.)

173 Bde R.F.A X. Corps 36. Division

Sept: 1918

Place	Date	Hour	Summary of Events and Information	Remarks and references to Appendices
			Ref. 28/40.000.	
			As Right Group of the Divisional Artillery the Brigade during the early part of the month followed the enemy in his retreat. We kept in close touch with the battalion we were supporting and did some useful work in knocking out machine guns, especially from the positions S.15 & T.14.	
			On several occasions good targets were obtained of the enemy in the open.	
			A considerable amount of material was salvaged from old Battery positions in the area lately occupied by the Brigade and this was found to be most useful when the batteries came into more or less permanent positions at NEUVE EGLISE.	
			The Brigade formed part of the Left Group of the 35th Divisional Artillery for the battle at YPRES 28 Sept: 1918, and on the afternoon of the same day was ordered to rejoin 36th Division & continue the advance.	
			Casualties during the early part of the month were slight in wounded men, but gas casualties were rather heavy.	
			The weather during the month was extremely variable and alternated between bright dry weather with strong winds, and very wet intervals - On the whole the weather was not altogether favorable for active operations.	

Army Form C. 2118.

WAR DIARY
or
INTELLIGENCE SUMMARY.
(Erase heading not required.)

173 Bde. R.F.A.

SEP. 1918

Place	Date	Hour	Summary of Events and Information	Remarks and references to Appendices
Sept.	1		Batteries in action in S.15.d and S.21.b.	
	2		Enemy H.V. guns strafed communications. Weather wet & rainy. Brigade Major wounded. Our casualties were heavy owing to enemy Machine Guns in Neuve Eglise.	
	3		Batteries took up forward positions in S.9. central. Remaining Batteries moved forward & took up positions in T.14.a, T.8.c and T.13.b. Brigade H.Q. being in T.14.a. Enemy used considerable gas shell and strafed the Neuve Eglise area very heavily. Hill 63 taken.	
	4		Division on our Right attack ROMARIN unsuccessfully. Enemy counter-attacked on the Northern slopes of Hill 63 & gained some ground. Weather fine & hot.	
	5		C/173rd Brigade & 407 Battery R.F.A. took up forward positions in T.9.C & T.9.d. Batteries were very heavily shelled with gas, especially B/173 Brigade R.F.A. who suffered considerable casualties.	

Army Form C. 2118.

WAR DIARY
or
INTELLIGENCE SUMMARY.
(Erase heading not required.)

173 Bde R.F.A

SEP. 1918.

Place	Date	Hour	Summary of Events and Information	Remarks and references to Appendices
Sep.	6.		A successful local attack North of GOOSEBERRY FARM, by which we gained Hill 49, with 30 to 40 prisoners – our casualties slight. Enemy Artillery quiet but gas shelling very heavy at night.	
	7		Weather changes to wet.	
	8		96th Brigade go out of action. Enemy fire very heavy. B/173 goes out of action to MOOTE BOOM. Simpson Group is dissolved and remaining three batteries of 173rd Bde go into the POTTER GROUP.	
	9		A/173 is moved to T.15.c.9.8 with forward sections in T.15.c. D/173 of Bde R.F.A forward Section in T.16.a	
	10.		Brigade Headquarters moved to R.15.b.7.9. Major R.R. SHARP, DSO, M.C., commands the Brigade from his battery position.	
	14		Adjutant 173rd Brigade acts for POTTER GROUP. H.Q. T.14.c. Enemy still using gas gas shell heavily in area shoots.	
	18.		Major SHARP takes command of the Group. 153rd Brigade R.F.A goes out of action. 2 batteries of 149 Brigade R.F.A come in. Gas shelling very heavy during the night.	

Army Form C. 2118.

WAR DIARY
or
INTELLIGENCE SUMMARY.
(Erase heading not required.)

173 Bde R.F.A

Title pages SEP. 1918

Instructions regarding War Diaries and Intelligence Summaries are contained in F. S. Regs., Part II. and the Staff Manual respectively. Title pages will be prepared in manuscript.

Place	Date	Hour	Summary of Events and Information	Remarks and references to Appendices
Sep.	19		Brigade goes out of action to Wagon Lines, being relieved by 149th Brigade R.F.A.	
	21		Brigade moved - wagon lines to G11d - Brigade H.Q. to H.8.e., and is attached to 157 Brigade of the 35th Division in the 2nd Corps. Half the guns go into action. Weather turns to wet.	
	23		Slight rain - coming operation postponed 72 hours until 28th Sept.	
	25		Weather fine.	
	27		Weather still remains fine with slight showers.	
	28		Battle started 6.15 am. Our batteries formed Left Group with two of the batteries of the 159th Brigade. Orders to move up to Wagon Lines in I.13.a at 5.0 pm, Headquarters being in the Laundry I.13.a.	
	29.		Brigade moved forward 5.0 am. C/173 Bde RFA moves into action at J.Y.d at 9.30 am. B/173 Bde RFA just North of C/173 at 11.0 am. A & D Batteries moved forward in the afternoon. Batteries did not shoot.	
	30.		Heavy rain all day. Batteries moved forward with great difficulty owing to the bad roads to J.29.a and to and go into action at 6.0 pm. in position in K27a & K26b, Headquarters being at TERHAN, K.15.c.	

Major R.F.A.
Commanding 173 Bde R.F.A.

Army Form C. 2118.

WAR DIARY
or
INTELLIGENCE SUMMARY.

173rd Brigade R.F.A.   X Corps.   36 Division.

OCTOBER 1918

Vol 36

Place	Date	Hour	Summary of Events and Information	Remarks and references to Appendices
			Reference 28/40,000 29/40,000	

As Right Group of the Divisional Artillery, the Brigade during the early part of the month was in Action South of TERHAND. In this period harassing fire amounting to 25 rounds per hour was kept up continuously.

Enemy artillery was very active, and the Brigade suffered considerable casualties in horses, especially in the forward wagon lines.

Owing to the shortage of material and the probability of an advance, very little could be done for the protection of battery positions, but in spite of this the Brigade suffered comparatively few casualties in personnel.

On the 14th of the month the Brigade took part in the advance and the capture of MOORSEELE, being relieved by the 41st Division on the 16th.

On the 18th the Brigade moved to the area East of LENDELEDE, and took part in the subsequent advance across the LYS, being finally relieved on the 27th October by the 34th Division, with batteries in action just West of KLEINHANEBEKE (29/J.7.) During the advance from TERHAND one battery of the Brigade was constantly in close touch with the battalion in the line. During the early period of the advance this work was carried out by A/173rd Bde R.F.A. under the Command of Major R.R. SHARP, D.S.O., M.C., and the later period by B/173rd Bde R.F.A. under the command of Major G.A. RICKARDS. M.C. Most excellent work was done by both these batteries with their forward guns, and they were undoubtedly of the very greatest assistance to the Infantry in overcoming hostile machine guns.

Major SHARP had a very successful shoot on a hostile 77 battery, destroying the personnel and enabling the Infantry to capture the guns. Observation for this was carried out from MOORSEELE which was practically in the front line for the time. This Officer also xxxxx on a forward reconnaissance with the help of an Infantry platoon, was instrumental in capturing over 40 of the enemy.

On relief by the 34th Division on the 28th October the Brigade marched down to the area between LAUWE and ROLLEGHEM, 29/N.31 and M.36.

Army Form C. 2118.

WAR DIARY
or
INTELLIGENCE SUMMARY.   173rd Brigade R.F.A.

(Erase heading not required.)

OCTOBER 1918

Instructions regarding War Diaries and Intelligence Summaries are contained in F. S. Regs., Part II. and the Staff Manual respectively. Title pages will be prepared in manuscript.

Place	Date	Hour	Summary of Events and Information	Remarks and references to Appendices
			Casualties to personnel during the month were slight, considering the active operations, but casualties to horses were rather heavy.	
			The weather was variable, but on the whole could not be described as altogether unfavorable for active operations. Towards the end of the month the weather was fine.	
	1		Brigade Headquarters at TERHAND 28/K.15.c. Batteries in action K.27.a and K.26.b.	
	2			
	3		An active policy of harassing fire was pursued.	
	4			
	5		Considerable casualties among horses.	
	6		153rd Brigade R.F.A., and 173rd Brigade R.F.A. form the SIMPSON GROUP of the Divisional artillery. Forward Positions chosen from 28/K.16.d. and K.17.c., and dumps made up to 250 rounds per gun in anticipation for attack on the 8th.	
	7			
	8			
	9		Enemy artillery very active in area shoots.	
	11		Attack on GOLDFLAKE FARM 28/L.19.c,07.22.	
	12		GOLDFLAKE FARM lost by the Infantry.	
	13		GOLDFLAKE FARM retaken. Guns go into action in positions as follows :- A/173, K.23.a. B/173 K.16.d., and C/173 & D/173 K.17.c. Brigade Headquarters K.17.d.	
	14		Battle started 05.30. MOORSEELE taken. A/173 goes forward with Left Battalion at 07.00 to L.22.b. Brigade Headquarters L.15.c.9.0. Batteries move forward to L.16.d. and L.16.a.	

A5834 Wt. W4973/M687 750,000 8/16 D. D. & L. Ltd. Forms/C.2118/13.

Army Form C. 2118.

WAR DIARY
or
INTELLIGENCE SUMMARY.

173rd Brigade R.F.A.

OCTOBER 1918

(Erase heading not required.)

Instructions regarding War Diaries and Intelligence Summaries are contained in F. S. Regs., Part II. and the Staff Manual respectively. Title pages will be prepared in manuscript.

Place	Date	Hour	Summary of Events and Information	Remarks and references to Appendices
	15		153rd Brigade R.F.A. ~~ceased to function in conjunction with 173rd Brigade R.F.A.~~ *goes out of the Support Group.* At 09.00 the Brigade fired a barrage for the Infantry to line of the LyS in COURTRAI. Headquarters at L.22.b., and at 15.00 moved again to 29/G.14.b. Batteries G.15.a. and b.	
	16		At 05.30 a barrage was started which was subsequently stopped as the Infantry had advanced into COURTRAI. The Brigade was relieved by the 41st Division in the afternoon. The Brigade draws out to 29/L.3.d. and L.9.b.	
	17		At Rest.	
	18		The Brigade moved - Headquarters to B.14.d., Batteries B.16.b., B.10.c. and d. Forward wagon lines move back to A.16.b.	
	19		Considerable enemy gas shelling and bombing during the night. The Brigade moved at 16.00 - Headquarters B.17.a., and Batteries in action B.18.	
	19/20		On the night 19/20th the 109th Infantry Brigade crosses the LyS. This Brigade covered these operations with a creeping barrage.	
	20		Advance by II Corps at 09.00 in co-operation with the French on the Left, and the 9th Division on the Right. (see appendix I)	App I
			108th Infantry Brigade goes through the 109th Infantry Brigade.	
	22		"A" and "B" batteries of the Brigade go to 107th Infantry Brigade at I.3.d. and I.9.a. 107th Infantry Brigade makes good progress on the Right. The rest of the Brigade crosses the LyS.	
	23		Brigade Headquarters at I.4.d. Batteries in action in I.11.a. and I.5.c. and d.	
	25		Operation in conjunction with the French and the 9th Division starts at 09.00. Batteries move forward to J.7.b. and d. Headquarters at I.12.d. (see Appendix II)	App II

Army Form C. 2118.

WAR DIARY
or
INTELLIGENCE SUMMARY.

(Erase heading not required.)

173rd Brigade R.F.A.

OCTOBER 1918

Place	Date	Hour	Summary of Events and Information	Remarks and references to Appendices
	25 (contd)		108th Infantry Brigade held up owing to French not advancing.	
			"A" "B" "C" batteries move back to rear positions during the night. Headquarters do not move.	
	27		The Brigade was relieved by 34th Division (see Appendix III)	App III
	28		The Brigade moved to new area.	
			ADDENDUM.	
			On the night of the 27th October "B" Battery was heavily shelled at KNOCK, one shell setting on fire the straw roof of the farm in which the battery was billeted. The Battery at once turned out to fight the fire. In a cellar under the burning building 25 civilians were sheltering who had covered the doorway with straw to keep out gas. This straw also caught fire and if it had not been for the Battery the whole of these civilians would probably have perished. A large amount of live stock was also got safely away. The work was made very difficult owing to the fact that the enemy was shelling the area with gas at the time, and the urgency was made far greater by the fact that a dump of German 8" shell with charges was placed just outside the burning building.	

Major R.F.A.
Commanding 173rd Brigade R.F.A.

Army Form C. 2118.

WAR DIARY
or
INTELLIGENCE SUMMARY.

173rd Brigade R.F.A.   XVth Corps
NOVEMBER 1918.   36th Division.

(Erase heading not required.)

Instructions regarding War Diaries and Intelligence Summaries are contained in F.S. Regs., Part II. and the Staff Manual respectively. Title pages will be prepared in manuscript.

Vol 34

Place	Date	Hour	Summary of Events and Information	Remarks and references to Appendices
				Reference 28/40,000. 29/40,000.
	1–8		During the early part of the month the Brigade remained at rest in the area between LAUWE and ROLLEGHEM, 29/N.31 and M.36.	
			On the 2nd November positions were reconnoitred in 29/P.21. and 27., but these were not occupied.	
	8		On the 8th the Brigade moved to new area North-east of BELLEGHEM in N.15. and 16. Positions were reconnoitred in P.32. and Guns were sent up to these positions on the 8th November, with full echelons of ammunition. Guards were also with the guns. The Brigade, however, remained at rest until Hostilities ceased, on the 11th November.	
			On the 12th the Brigade moved to new area in TOURCOING, 28/X.23.	
			The Divisional Artillery was inspected by the Corps Commander on the 2nd of the month.	
			Casualties to Men or Horses during the month were nil.	
	11		The weather was wet and variable up to the 11th. After that it was fine until towards the end of the month, when it became variable again.	
	12–30		The brigade at rest between LAUWE and ROLLEGHEM.	
			Moved to N.15 and 16 North-east of BELLEGHEM.	
			Hostilities ceased at 11.00 hours.	
			The Brigade at TOURCOING. 28/X.23.	
			A program of Training, Education and Sports inaugurated and proceeded with.	

1.12.18

H.E.B.
Lieut Col R.F.A.
Commanding 173rd Bde R.F.A.

WAR DIARY
or
INTELLIGENCE SUMMARY.
(Erase heading not required.)

173rd Brigade R.F.A. XV Corps. 36th Division.

FEBRUARY 1919.

Place	Date	Hour	Summary of Events and Information	Remarks references Appendices
	1.		Brigade at TOURCOING.	
	20.		Demobilization of Men and Horses continued.	
	22.3.19.		Brigade ordered to be reduced to Cadre "A".	

Commanding 173rd Brigade R.F.A.

Lieut.Col. R.F.A.

www.ingramcontent.com/pod-product-compliance
Lightning Source LLC
Chambersburg PA
CBHW080850230426
43662CB00013B/2066

Army Form C. 2118.

WAR DIARY
or
INTELLIGENCE SUMMARY.

173rd Bde R.F.A.
XVth Corps.
36th Division.

Title pages DECEMBER 1918.

(Erase heading not required.)

Place	Date	Hour	Summary of Events and Information	Remarks and references to Appendices
	1. G. 30.		BRIGADE AT TOURCOING.	
	1.		Programme of Training, Recreation and Sports continued.	
	7.		Demobilization of Miners commenced.	
	17.2.19.		H.B.	

Commanding, 173rd Brigade, R.F.A.
Lieut.Col. R.F.A.

Army Form C. 2118.

WAR DIARY
or
INTELLIGENCE SUMMARY.

173rd Brigade R.F.A.   XVth Corps.   36th Division.

(Erase heading not required.)

Place	Date	Hour	Summary of Events and Information	Remarks and references to Appendices
Brigade at TOURCOING.	1.		Programme of Training, Recreation and Sports continued.	
	6.30.			
	4.		Demobilization of Pivotal, Guaranteed Letter and Long Service Men continued.	
	7.		Demobilization of Miners Continued.	
	23.		First consignment of Horses left this Brigade for Demobilization.	

JANUARY 1919.

17.2.19.

H.E.B.

Lieut.Col.R.F.A.
Commanding.173rd Brigade R.F.A.